Greeks and Parthians
in Mesopotamia and Beyond

GREEKS AND PARTHIANS
IN MESOPOTAMIA
AND BEYOND

331 BC – 224 AD

Wolfram Grajetzki

Bristol Classical Press

First published in 2011 by
Bristol Classical Press
an imprint of
Bloomsbury Academic
Bloomsbury Publishing Plc
36 Soho Square,
London W1D 3QY, UK

CIP records for this book are available from the
British Library and the Library of Congress

ISBN 978-0-7156-3947-4

Typeset by Ray Davies

www.bloomsburyacademic.com

Contents

Part 1. The Historical Setting

Part 2. The Places

Acknowledgements

I am grateful to Paul Whelan for his drawing of the Greek statue found at Seleucia, to Sally-Ann Ashton for comments on an early draft of the book, to Stephen Quirke for commenting on my English, to Deborah Blake for accepting the book for publication and editing the text, and to Ray Davies for the typesetting and layout.

List of Illustrations and Sources

Drawings are by the author unless
otherwise stated.

Introduction

This book follows the development of urban life in Babylonia, Elymais and the northern part of the Persian Gulf, from the arrival of Alexander the Great (331 BC) to the end of the Parthian empire (224 AD). For this period of about 500 years, certain cities have been selected as our access to the people living and working in the region as a whole. The heartland of the most ancient civilisations, this area remained throughout these centuries, as it still is today, a region of immense political and cultural importance. After the collapse of the Persian empire with the conquest of Alexander the Great around 330 BC, the region saw dramatic changes. This book will explore aspects of these new developments, and consider how the political events affected the lives of people of all classes, with particular attention to the archaeological evidence. Much has been written on the period, but mainly focussing on single aspects rather than aiming to provide a general picture.

The first two hundred years are dominated by the rule of the Seleucids, the Greek-speaking dynasty founded by one of Alexander's generals. In the second century BC, the Parthians, a central Asian tribe, took control of one Seleucid province, and later of most of the others, creating an empire which lasted for almost 450 years. Several books have been published on Parthian history and art, but many historians treat the period as a time of decline, especially compared to the later Sassanian and earlier Achaemenid empires. Two reasons in particular may account for such negative views. First, the political history of the Parthian empire superficially offers little in the way of great events or personalities. It seems to have been a loose federal state, continually involved in civil war, and in the first and second centuries AD always on the defensive against the Romans. Secondly, Parthian art is too often seen as a degenerate version of Greek art, lacking true understanding of its rules and principles. This view is clearly expressed by the important Iranian scholar Ernst Herfzfeld.[1] The major study of Parthian sculpture states that 'Parthian art is not original to any great extent'.[2] Another important book on the Parthians declares of their art in the later second and early third century: 'Parthian art seemingly went rotten at the centre'.[3] Even as recently as 2005 an author can mention the scale of buildings of the Parthians, but see in them 'a touch of nouveau riche'.[4] This is almost certainly meant as a negative comment, although sociologists might argue that the presence of the 'nouveau riche' is a sign

1

of an open society with opportunities for those outside the established nobility. However, different views on Parthian art were expressed even in early studies. In 1934 Fritz Wirth described the façade of a Parthian palace excavated in Assur as 'elegant'.[5] Daniel Schlumberger also came to a much more positive view, emphasising that Parthian art is Oriental and cannot be judged by western standards.[6]

It is certainly possible to provide a more balanced picture of the Parthian empire. It lasted almost half a millennium, so not everything about it can have been bad or going wrong. Parthian art, with its frontalism, is remarkably similar to later Byzantine and mediaeval art, and could therefore be seen as highly influential for the next thousand years of art history. In architecture the stucco decorations and the *iwan* – a hall with one open side – were highly influential on Islamic architecture. Parthian art seems Oriental after the experience of Greek art.

The Seleucid Greeks are relatively well known, as many ancient historians wrote about them. However, there are no extant historical works compiled by a Seleucid writer. The information on their kings is often indirect, and comes from their opponents, most notably the Romans. However, there are many archaeological sources that can provide further information and correct the negative view provided by their foes.

The same is true for the Parthians. The history of this people presents still more problems and questions. Their own literature, with any history writing, is entirely lost, and we know them again principally from their main enemies, the Romans. The focus of this book is therefore on life as reflected in archaeological sources of this region of the world from about 320 BC – 224 AD. A feature of both Seleucid and Parthian empires was a marked lack of centralisation. Many regions were ruled by local governors of indigenous, not Greek or Parthian origin. Everywhere local traditions remained visibly strong, and were, at least in case of the Seleucids, supported by the state. In the Parthian period the local character of individual regions can still be detected, but now submerged under a new general trend. Now, at least on the surface, the empire became more Hellenised than under the Hellenistic rulers of the Seleucid Dynasty.

The regions covered by this book are the vassal kingdoms of Characene and Elymais, and the southern part of Mesopotamia in general, better known as Babylonia. These provinces circle the north-western end of the Gulf, which became increasingly important at this time because of the maritime trade with India. This is certainly one of the most important regions of the Parthian empire. Previously studies on Parthian culture, especially on art, have tended to focus on centres such as Hatra or Dura Europos, but these lay at the edge of the area under their control. New excavations and publications over the last 30 years now make it possible to write more about the centre of the empire, especially in terms of culture and daily life.

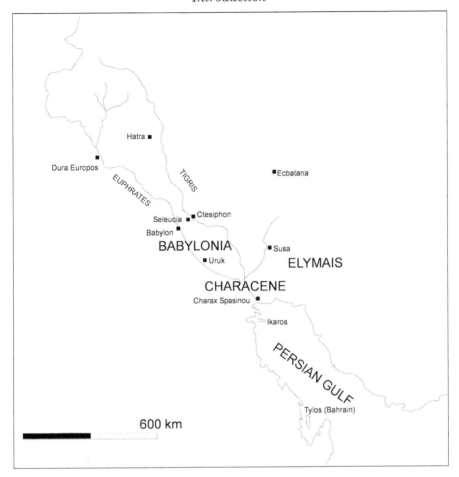

Fig. 1. Map of the region: the Persian Gulf and southern Mesopotamia.

Climate and geography

The south of Mesopotamia is an alluvial land: the soil that makes up the fields has been deposited by the rivers Euphrates and Tigris. Over thousands of years they have brought silt down to the sea, creating new land on the shores of the Gulf. One example that illustrates the process is Charax Spasinou, the capital of Characene. It was built as a sea port, but only a few hundred years after its foundation it must have lain a certain distance from the shore, as a new port, Forat, was established about 17 kilometres away. Both places are today over 100 kilometres inland. Across the entire region climate is generally intensely hot, and was described as such by ancient writers (e.g. Strabo XVI, 4, 1). The summers are long and humid. Rain falls only in the short winter, from December to February, when there is occasional frost. However, the region is also fertile, suitable for agriculture and viticulture, as well as several types of fruit. The main city in the region was Charax Spasinou, founded by Alexander the Great. In the north Uruk and Babylon were the two greatest ancient cities. Both still retained some importance in the Seleucid and Parthian period.

In the Gulf, Bahrain was the most important island, most likely always belonging to Characene and therefore indirectly also to the Parthian empire. Its political position under the preceding Seleucid rule is not certain. The island covers an area of about 570 square kilometers. Bahrain has an extreme summer, with a relatively mild winter. There is little rainfall, and about 90% of the island is covered by desert. Whether the coast of Saudi Arabia also belonged to the Seleucid and Parthian empires and to Characene is so far unknown. There are not many recorded archaeological sites, and few of them have been researched.

Elymais forms the core region of the ancient Kingdom of Elam. The climate and geography are significantly different from those of Mesopotamia. The northern part is characterised by many mountains: the Zagros mountain system is a chain of deeply folded, high rising rock masses with fertile valleys between. The climate is continental, with cold winters and hot summers. Land suitable for cultivation is found between the mountains in the valleys. There are also extensive woodlands. The southern part, a plain also known as Khuzistan, is more an extension of south Mesopotamia, but again with a more continental climate (hot summers, cold winters). This area is divided by several rivers, and Susa is its main city.

Although trade was an essential part of the Seleucid and Parthian economies, there is no doubt that agriculture was the economic basis of society. Cereal crops, rice, fruit and vegetables were important. Several wine accounts are preserved, demonstrating the importance of viticulture. Domestic animals were also prominent in the economy: sheep, goats, cattle, pigs, horses, asses and camels were all present.

Dating systems

In 312 BC the Greek general Seleucus I conquered Babylon in the aftermath of the struggles over the empire of Alexander the Great. The victory was treated as historically important and marks the beginning of a new era in a chronological system used not only by the Greeks in the east, but also by the Parthians and other people in western Asia for many centuries. Many coins of the rulers in this region are dated by this era, and these provide a relatively secure guideline for its chronology. The Parthians themselves also introduced a dating system, the royal Arsacid era. Like the Seleucid one, it was counted from the spring onwards, beginning from 247 BC. Arsacid year 1 (247 BC) might refer to the time when the first Parthian king Arsaces ascended the throne.[7] Many documents have double datings, using both systems side by side.

Part 1

The Historical Setting

The Seleucids in Mesopotamia

In a military campaign almost without parallel in ancient history, the Macedonian king Alexander the Great conquered Syria, Egypt, Mesopotamia, Persia and India. The last Persian king, Darius III, was finally defeated in the battle of Gaugamela (331 BC), a place not yet securely located, but perhaps somewhere in the north of Mesopotamia. From the beginning, Alexander the Great intended to make Mesopotamia the centre of his world empire and to promote Babylon to its capital. He aimed to unify Greek and Persian culture and society. By 324 he was in Babylon, but he died in 323 at the age of 32.

After Alexander's death his generals fought for control of the huge empire he had left behind. The first governor of the Asian provinces was Perdiccas, a former general and friend of Alexander's. He managed to suppress a revolt of Greeks in the far east of the empire.[1] However, he was murdered in 321 on a military campaign against Egypt. Antigonus Monophthalmus, another of Alexander's generals, followed him as ruler of the Asian provinces. Under his rule, yet another of Alexander's generals, Seleucus, became the governor of the province of Babylonia. In 316 he was driven out by Antigonus, but managed to acquire the support of the local population by respecting their customs. In 312 he reconquered Babylon, and in 311 a peace treaty was concluded between the two men. In the following years Seleucus I took over most of the eastern part of Alexander's empire, more or less covering the territories of modern Iraq and Iran. Antigonus ruled in the area of modern Turkey, with the Euphrates as border. However, in 301 he was defeated in a new war with Seleucus, whose ally Lysimachus received Turkey. In this way, Seleucus succeeded in extending his empire over Syria as well.

The empire established by Seleucus I encompassed by far the largest part of the territories conquered by Alexander the Great, and certainly the most diverse. People of many different ethnic origins, speaking many different languages, lived in this new kingdom, which stretched from India in the east, over modern Iran and Iraq to Syria in the west. Greeks also now arrived in great numbers, adding another ethnic minority to this mix of people. Seleucia on the Tigris, not far from modern Baghdad, was founded as the empire's capital. Another capital, Antioch, was established in Syria shortly afterwards, providing the empire with two focal points. Antioch was situated very much in the west, close to the Mediterranean, demonstrating the links of the Greeks to their home lands. Its location perhaps also underlined the dominant orientation of their politics towards the west rather than the east, where there was the powerful Indian empire with its utterly different cultural roots. Seleucia on the Tigris stood more in the heartland of the empire, but in the overall picture still within its western half. Another royal residence, though most likely not of the same importance, was Ecbatana, in modern Iran. The city functioned throughout the Seleucid period and into the Parthian period as an important mint for the coinage of the kingdom, but little is known of its architecture in these later periods.

For the administration of his empire Seleucus I took over the system in force under the Persians. The latter had divided it into several provinces, called satrapies. Seleucus did not change this arrangement, but new satrapies were installed. Mesopotamia was divided into the two satrapies Assyria (in the north) and Babylonia (south). To the east was the satrapy called Elymais.

Seleucus I was succeeded by his son Antiochus I (281-261 BC). For most of his reign, he was involved in a series of wars in the west. In turn, his son Antiochus II ruled from 261 to 246 BC. He again fought in the west, especially against the strong kingdom of Egypt, ruled by the successors of Ptolemy, yet another of Alexander the Great's generals. However, in the east, the huge empire started to fall apart, as it was simply too big to be controlled. In antiquity travel by land was extremely slow, and so speed of communication within such a large area was always a problem for the central authority. Unlike the Roman empire, arranged around the Mediterranean with travel by sea serving as swifter communication system, the Seleucid empire was very much an inland realm. It must always have taken a long time to transfer messages from one end to the other and back. In such a vast territory, rebels would have had enough time to establish their rule and assemble all means of support before an army from the central government could act, or any other kind of further help arrive. Indeed, Bactria, the most eastern satrapy of the Seleucid empire, declared independence under a certain Diodotus I, who was most likely a former governor who became king and minted his own coins. At about the same time, around 250 BC, the Parthian satrapy under the Parmi did the same with their king Arsaces I.

Seleucus II and Seleucus III were again more heavily involved in wars against the west. At least these wars are fairly well recorded in our sources. Antiochus III, also called Antiochus the Great, ruled from 223 to 187 BC. He is regarded as the last important king of the Seleucid empire, although his successes were not really stable and did not last longer than one generation after his death. Antiochus III is well known for his military campaigns, one leading him to the east, where he fought against the Bactrian Greeks and the Parthians. For a short period the Parthians were forced to accept Seleucid rule, but then Antiochus III started to fight wars in the west again, giving the Parthians in turn a new opportunity to

Fig. 2. Head of Seleucus I.

become an independent kingdom. Antiochus III also led a campaign against Arabia, targeting Gerrha, evidently an important city and maybe the centre of an empire. It is likely that Bahrain became part of the Seleucid empire as a result of this campaign.

Shortly before the reign of Antiochus III, several new satrapies were introduced. Paropotamia was a new district along the Middle Euphrates, separated from Babylonia. The south of Babylonia became the satrapy of the Erythraean Sea, as the southernmost part of Mesopotamia. Information about this second new province is scarce. In 221 BC Pythiadas is mentioned as governor (*eparchos*). He was succeeded by Tychon, who was set in place by Antiochus III after a certain Molon had occupied the whole region in rebellion against the king.[2]

The exact size of the satrapy of the Erythraean Sea is not certain, but the islands Failaka and Bahrain were most likely parts of it, as they were later also part of the kingdom of Characene which developed from this satrapy. The capital, later Charax, was at this time called Alexandria.

After Antiochus III the empire rapidly fell apart. Antiochus IV (175-164 BC) was the last king who tried to take control over the Iranian provinces.

Fig. 3. Portrait of
Antiochus IV on a coin.

He was extremely short of money and decided to loot a temple of Artemis in the Elymais. The locals resisted and the enterprise failed. The king died on his way home. Under Demetrius I (162-150 BC) Mesopotamia and Media rebelled. When Demetrius I came to power, the satrap of Media, Timarchus, did not acknowledge the new king, but declared himself king and minted his own coins. He seized Mesopotamia. However, in winter 161/0 Demetrius I was able to defeat and kill this rebel king. He celebrated himself as heir to the legacy of Alexander the Great. Coins minted in Seleucia on the Tigris show him – like Alexander the Great – crowned with an elephant scalp.[3] However, under Alexander I Balas (150-145 BC) and Antiochus VI (144-141 BC) Seleucid rule in Iran and Mesopotamia finally collapsed. In summer 148 Elymais was still part of the Seleucid empire, as one dated inscription shows, but by 141 the Parthian king Mithridates I, coming from the north, had conquered the capital Seleucia on the Tigris. Shortly after 140, Elymais with Susa must have fallen to the Parthians.[4] Not surprisingly, the Greek population of the conquered cities sought help from the new Seleucid king Demetrius II (145-138 and later 129-125 BC). He arrived with an army, but was captured and imprisoned by the Parthians in 138.[5]

Antiochus VII (138-129 BC) was the last Seleucid king to attempt to gain control over Mesopotamia. In 131 he marched with 80,000 men from Antioch against Mesopotamia. Many local rulers and people welcomed him. Perhaps in June 131 he achieved success in one great battle and two smaller ones against the Parthian governor Indates. Antiochus conquered Babylon, where he spent the winter of 131/0. In spring 130 the Parthian king Phraates II asked for a peace treaty. He himself was involved in heavy fighting on the eastern border of his kingdom, and was keen to keep the western frontier quiet. Antiochus VII demanded Mesopotamia, most of Iran, high tribute and, finally, the return of his brother Demetrius II, still a Parthian hostage. Altogether this was too much, and Phraates II refused his demands. Now, Antiochus VII went further. He reached Susa and in 130 conquered Ecbatana. In winter 130/29 he placed troops there in several Iranian towns and cities. The local population had to feed these soldiers; furthermore, the Seleucid forces treated the local population badly, and any sympathy they had for the Seleucids was lost. In February/

March 129, with the support of the local population, the Parthian army attacked the Seleucids in their winter quarters. Antiochus VII died in the fighting and his son Seleucus was captured. Phraates II was on the point of launching an invasion of Syria, as the Seleucid main province was without an army. However, there was an uprising of his Scythian troops, and he was not able to proceed with his Syrian enterprise. The Parthian king arranged a royal burial for the Seleucid king, as Alexander the Great had done for the Persian king Darius III. This military campaign was the last Seleucid effort to reconquer Mesopotamia. The Seleucid empire was reduced to a local kingdom in Syria and finally disappeared in 63 BC with the Roman conquest of Syria.[6]

A brief history of the Parthians

It is difficult to write a history of the Parthians, as no work of Parthian literature has been preserved[7] and most of the information available about them was written by their enemies, most often the Greeks and Romans, generally casting the Parthians in an extremely negative light. These written histories also concentrate on military history and the battles between the Parthians and their neighbours, while other events are given little attention or not mentioned at all. Therefore, periods where there are no serious conflicts are not well documented, while periods of war and trouble with the west are quite well known. The periods without wars in particular may have been times of prosperity and stability. Nevertheless the beginning of Parthian history is described in detail by the ancient Roman writer Pompeius Trogus, who wrote a world history in 44 books. His original work is lost, but the third-century author Justin compiled a summary, which is preserved.[8]

Parthia is a region in the north of present-day Iran, to the east of the Caspian Sea. The region is first mentioned in Achaemenid times as one of the satrapies of this empire. Not much is known about the history of the region under the Seleucid empire. The first governor was Nicanor; little is known about him.

According to Pompeius Trogus[9] there was a tribe called Parni living near the Caspian Sea. They were one of three tribes in the confederacy of the Dahae, which lived in the same region. In a wider sense these were most likely among the nomadic peoples named in earlier Greek histories as Scythians.[10] Around the middle of the third century BC, the satrap (governor) Andragoras ruled in Parthia. He started a rebellion against the Seleucid rule, but was overthrown by the Parni, who killed him and themselves took control of Parthia. This was around 247 BC. This date is the starting point of the Parthian calendar and therefore it has been assumed that this was the date of the founding of the new state. Some ancient historians add that the Parni had already lived for a long time in the province before revolting against the Seleucids.[11] If so, it is possible

9

that they had long since lost their nomadic lifestyle, and were familiar with Greek traditions.

The first known king was Arsaces, who became such a prominent figure of Parthian history that the name 'Arsaces' was in later times the title of the Parthian kings, in the same way as 'Caesar' or 'Augustus' became titles for Roman emperors. In administrative texts the Parthian kings are often called simply 'Arsaces' and not identified by their proper name. Little is known about Arsaces I and his successors. However, the survival of the small kingdom in its early phase was certainly threatened from the outside. Obviously the Seleucid kings attacked them and tried to re-conquer the lost province, but Parthia was far from the political centres of the Seleucid empire, and the Greek rulers seem to have been much more involved in fighting in the west – at least this is the impression we have from our (western) sources. The turning point comes with Phraates I who ruled from about 176 to 171 BC. At this time the Seleucids were again embroiled in several wars in the west, which were partly successful but still weakened their power. Phraates I ruled only for a short time, but managed to attack Seleucid provinces around the Caspian Sea and conquer them.[12] His successor, Mithridates I (*c.* 171-139/8 BC), is often called the true founder of the Parthian empire. In a series of campaigns he managed to overcome large parts of what is now Iran, and finally he conquered Mesopotamia, where in this period Greek rule was rather weak. Mithridates I called himself 'Philhellene' ('lover of Greeks'), demonstrating his orientation towards Greek culture and perhaps towards the Greeks in his empire, who held many key positions. The Greeks most likely made up a high proportion of the ruling classes in his empire, and it was therefore wise to seek their support.[13] On his coins he calls himself 'of Arsaces', 'of king Arsaces' and finally 'of the great King Arsaces'.[14] The precise timing of his conquests is poorly known. Between 160 and 155 BC he conquered parts of the east. In 148/7 he took over Media, where a certain Bakasis became governor. From there he went north to the Caspian Sea, and then south. By July 141 BC he was in Seleucia on the Tigris. Shortly afterwards he defeated the Seleucid governor of Babylonia, and in 140 BC he was in Susa.[15]

The Seleucid empire was now in a state of disintegration. Especially in Mesopotamia, the following years brought constant wars for supremacy, which continued for almost two decades. Several local governors made themselves kings and fought for control in Mesopotamia and Iran. In this period, the provinces Characene (most of southern Mesopotamia) and Elymais (western Iran) declared independence, but were unable to hold on to it for long (see pp. 18, 25). Demetrios II, the Seleucid king, responded by marching into Mesopotamia. After initial success, he was finally captured, put in chains and paraded through several towns and regions which had supported the Seleucids. Finally the king was brought to Hyrcania (an

Iranian province near the Caspian Sea), where he married Rhodogune, a daughter of Mithridates I.[16]

Mithridates I died about 139/8 BC. He had transformed the small Parthian kingdom into a vast empire, stretching from the borders of Bactria (modern Afghanistan) in the east to Mesopotamia in the west. Together with the Roman and the Chinese empires, it was now one of the largest empires of its day.

Mithridates I was followed on the throne by his son Phraates II. The Seleucid king Antiochus VII attacked him in the west and was able to re-conquer Babylon, certainly one of the key cities of the region (see pp. 46-7), but was finally defeated by Phraates II. Meanwhile, in the east, tribes coming from Central Asia destroyed the Greek empire of Bactria and began to threaten the young Parthian empire. The events in the east are especially badly recorded in surviving histories. However, we hear that Phraates II was killed on the eastern front by Greeks taken as prisoners in the wars in the west, who immediately turned against him when the army came in contact with the enemy.[17] His successor, Artabanus I, also died in the battles against the eastern invaders, demonstrating how difficult and unstable the situation was.

In 124/3 BC Mithridates II, son of Artabanus I, became king and retook Mesopotamia, where the situation was not yet consolidated. He attacked Armenia in the north and was finally able to stabilise the eastern provinces. It seems that the young empire was saved. He is the first Parthian king to be called 'king of the kings' on coins[18] and in cuneiform texts.[19] Characene was made into a vassal kingdom. It was still ruled by its own kings, but had to except Parthian supremacy. This seems a deliberate strategy for ruling the new empire. The vassal kingdoms acted independently on some levels, making it perhaps less likely that they would rebel against the central government. On the other hand, they certainly had to pay some kind of taxes, besides perhaps assisting the central government in military matters, such as supplying soldiers or maybe just food while an army crossed the vassal state. The Parthian kings sometimes even placed members of their own family as kings in these vassal kingdoms, a practice best known from Armenia, but partly also from Characene. The Parthian empire therefore operated as a kind of federal state. There was always the danger that the vassal kingdoms might turn against the central government, but in general, their semi-independence seems to have guaranteed greater stability. In case of military attacks from outside, the vassal kingdoms were able to organise some resistance on their own. Even when the Parthian capital was conquered, this decentralisation ensured that another part of the empire still functioned and could mobilise a counter attack. This system may have been one reason why the empire lasted longer than the Achaemenid and the Sassanian empires, and was in this respect more successful.[20]

Also under Mithridates II the Parthians came into contact with the

Romans for the first time. Mithridates II made a treaty with them, fixing the Euphrates as the border of the two empires. In his reign, too, the Silk Road was opened. From Chinese sources, we know that at about this time a delegation from China reached the Parthian empire.[21] From now on, there were constant trade relations between China and the Parthian empire and even beyond. At the end of his long reign (*c.* 124/3-88/7 BC) Mithridates II had to fight against a rebel king Gotarzes I who ruled in Babylonia, a key province of the empire; the rebellion was eventually suppressed a decade later. Mithridates II is perhaps the most important Parthian ruler. While the earlier kings had expanded the borders of the empire, he achieved the same but also consolidated Parthian rule. Not much is known about the politics of his rule, but there are signs that at the end of his reign many things changed. Up to his time cuneiform was still being used in the administration. This ceased during his reign, after which the ancient script appears only in religious and scientific texts. Architecture also underwent a change: the great Mesopotamian-style temple complexes at Uruk burned down. Whether or not this relates to civil wars, it is significant that they were not rebuilt in the old style; rather, new temple buildings were erected in Parthian style. This might relate to a reorganisation of the temple administration. Maybe other types of administration replaced the old oriental-style temple organisation.[22]

For the following years, little is known about Parthian history. There is evidence for civil wars, with at least two kings reigning at the same time. This period of unrest ended with Orodes II (58/7-38 BC), under whom the Romans attacked the Parthians for the first time on a larger scale. For far-away Rome, the Parthians perhaps seemed nothing more than a tribe, like many others. It is uncertain whether the Romans had any idea of the size of the Parthian empire or its strength, and it seems that they misjudged its power. The climax of the invasion was an epoch-making battle between the Romans and the Parthians in 53 BC. The general of the Parthians appears in classical sources as Surena, who became an almost legendary figure in later Persian sources. The Romans were routed in what became infamous in their history as the 'battle of Carrhae', one of the

Fig. 4. Coin of Orodes II.

Fig. 5. Coin of Musa and Phraates V.

heaviest military disasters in Roman history. About 20,000 Romans were killed and 10,000 captured. Crassus, the Roman general, was slain and his head brought to the Parthian king.[23] One reason for the Parthian success was the 'Parthian shot' described by Plutarch, who wrote a biography of Crassus. The 'Parthian shot' was a military tactic, perhaps already developed by the Scythians and other Eurasian nomads. While an army attacked the Parthian cavalry they turned away, making the attacker believe that they were retreating. Indeed, they were shooting backwards while riding away from the enemy, thus confusing the attackers who assumed they had already won. In 38 BC Phraates IV succeeded his father Orodes II as king. In his reign, the Parthians again inflicted a massive defeat on the Romans, this time led by their general Mark Antony (Marcus Antonius). Again, some 10,000 Romans were killed. The Romans now recognised the Parthians as another world power.

Over the following hundred years the Parthian empire seems to have been quite stable. We hear constantly of small-scale fighting against the Romans, and about some dynastic troubles, but the empire did not lose much of its territory, even though it did not expand further. At least once, a woman ruled over the Parthian empire. Female rulers are known from Hellenistic courts, but not otherwise for the Parthians. The ruling queen was Musa, who reigned from 2 BC to 2 AD with her son Phraates, also called 'Phraatakes ('little Phraates').[24] She is one of the few Parthian queens known by name.[25] Archaeology reveals that Babylonia and the region around Susa flourished in this period, enjoying a level of prosperity not known before or since.

It is often stated that with Alexander the Great much changed in the Near East, not only politically but also in terms of material culture. According to this view, there is a great dividing line in the archaeology, by which everything can be classified as before or after Alexander. However, the evidence is certainly not that easy to interpret. Indeed, in many places nothing changed after Alexander the Great. Old Babylonian traditions continued unbroken, and it seems that Greek or Hellenised places were simply islands in a Mesopotamian world. The major changes in fact come only after the Parthians. They, rather than their Greek predecessors, were the rulers who transformed Mesopotamian art, architecture and many parts of life. Under the Seleucids some of the largest Babylonian-style temples were built, and cuneiform was still used in the administration. All this disappears gradually under the Parthians. Temples were now built in a new hybrid style, using Greek forms but with a different aesthetic. The same applies to sculpture and painting. A marked frontalism appears, not known from Babylonian paintings but always there in sculpture. The turning point is perhaps the middle of the first century AD. Around this time most of material culture changed from both the Greek and the Mesopotamian traditions to what we call Parthian. This is visible in the pottery style[26] as much as in sculpture, where in the first century BC frontal heads became common.[27] These changes can be compared with developments in the Roman world. In particular, one contemporary parallel may be mentioned: Ptolemaic to Roman Egypt. Under the Ptolemies (305-30 BC), Greeks lived in Egypt, but largely segregated: there is little evidence that they affected the religious and material culture of the Egyptians. After the Roman conquest of Egypt in 30 BC, Egyptian-style temples continued to be built, but otherwise, the culture of daily life became Hellenised. By the end of the first century AD, domestic life in every region had been fully transformed, and the old Egyptian culture survived only in some areas of religious practice.

Even at the beginning of Parthian history, the culture of the Parthian court was much influenced by Greek culture. This should not come as a surprise. Greeks ruled and influenced countries as far east as India for about two hundred years. Greek was the language of the central administration and Greek artists and craftsmen dominated the material culture of the royal court. Inscriptions on Parthian coins were in Greek, and the dating most often followed the Greek Seleucid Era. At local level, by contrast, there seem to have been different developments, building on traditions going back to the fourth millennium BC. For writing, several centres were still using cuneiform script, introduced originally by the Sumerians before 3000 BC, and at certain places the Aramaic language and script continued to be used, as they had been under the Achaemenid empire.

At first sight, this change of style in the Parthian empire seems extraordinary: it was not the Greeks, but the Iranian Parthians, who introduced Hellenistic forms. However, the Parthians may have been much more widely accepted by local populations as indigenous rulers, not invaders (as the Greeks were regarded). From early on they presented themselves as Iranians.[28] Although they also invaded from the outside there seems never to have been a marked difference between them and the indigenous people. Parthian style could thus have been regarded as indigenous too, paving the way for its adoption in all parts of the empire. In terms of architecture, arts and lifestyle, in 150 BC most places in Mesopotamia and Iran must have still felt not very different from the time of the Babylonians around

Fig. 6. Coins of Artabanus II, minted in Seleucia.

500 BC. By 50 AD the picture had changed completely. Arts, crafts and architecture were transformed to a new style, superficially close to that of Greek and Roman world, but in detail substantially different in ways that would prove highly innovative for Byzantine and mediaeval art. It is clear that with the Parthians something new began.

One further reason for the acceptance of the new style might be the political fragmentation of the Parthian empire. Local kings acted more or less independently. They adopted the arts and culture of the ruling court, not because they were forced to do so, but following the 'court fashions' of a regime that was not seen as an enemy. Another reason might be an influx of new peoples, perhaps on a greater scale than the earlier Greek settlers. At Dura Europos, in the north of Mesopotamia, many inscriptions and documents of the Parthian period have been found. These show a mixture of languages, names and religions, including Jews, Greeks, and people speaking Aramaic and Syrian. There was a synagogue, a Christian church and temples to Syrian and Greek gods. All these were decorated in Parthian style. Under the Seleucids there had been few signs of the fusion of Greek and Oriental culture, which happens only under the Parthians. As already mentioned, by the end of the first century AD there are indications that the Parthians had moved away from purely Greek traditions. At just this time, the Roman emperors were cultivating their Hellenic heritage more than ever before, and the contrast suggests that Parthian art might even be seen as a reaction against the Romans and their insistently Hellenistic heritage. However, there are too few archaeological sites known where the development is clearly visible. Therefore many questions remain over the beginning of the new Parthian style.

Artabanus II (10/1-38 AD) had a long and important reign, consolidating the empire after a period of inner unrest. He seems to have been involved in many successful wars,[29] but Roman accounts also report problems within the empire.[30] In the east, parts of the empire might have been lost at this time. Here an Indo-Parthian empire appeared[31] alongside a new world power, the Kushan empire. At the Parthian court itself, the arts, especially the coins, give the impression that Hellenistic traditions lost their importance. Significantly, the Parthian king is no longer called 'philhellene'.[32]

One particular episode of rural unrest is known from the reign of Artabanus II. Thanks to the account of the Jewish historian Josephus Flavius, this is one of the best documented such uprisings for the whole of ancient history.[33] Little is known about the social structure of the Parthian empire. There was certainly a small ruling class, consisting of locals from various ethnic backgrounds. Traders and craftsmen perhaps formed some kind of middle class. The bulk of the population comprised those directly involved in food production, the farmers living in the countryside and in the towns and cities. According to Justin there were, below the king 'councillors' (*ordo probulorum*), who could became leaders (*duces*) in war, but also politicians (*rectores*) in peace times. There were slaves (*servi*) and freemen (*liberi*).[34]

Under Artabanus II two Jewish brothers, Anilaios and Asinaios, left their home town Neardea and turned to banditry and racketeering. They built a stronghold from which they soon became so wealthy that the Parthian satrap of the region moved against them, but he was defeated in battle. Their rapid rise could only have been possible with the support of many locals, presumably unhappy with their own living conditions. It seems that many of their supporters were also Jews, perhaps struggling economically and hoping for a better life. After the defeat of the satrap, the brothers were summoned to the royal court, where Artabanus II granted them freedom, because he feared revolt by other satraps and was hoping that the two brothers could provide support against such potential rebels. As a result, they formed a kind of vassal state within Babylonia. The events are certainly related to social conditions, and their success best explained by the impoverished background of many people joining the two brothers. However, they did not found any political movement to improve social conditions in general. Instead we hear that they were active for some fifteen years, looting villages of the region. Finally, after the death of Asinaios, the local population turned against his brother Anilaios and killed him.[35]

The reign of Vologases I (51-76/80 AD) saw the minting of the first coins with Aramaic inscriptions, and the founding of a royal city called Vologesias. The new city might have been founded to remove inhabitants from the still Greek city Seleucia, always a strong political centre, and often in opposition to the ruling king. An earlier king Vardanes (38-45 AD) had already established his residence in Ctesiphon, next to Seleucia, perhaps also to demonstrate his opposition to the Greeks, especially in this city.

In the written sources, the second century AD appears as a time of steady decline for the Parthian empire. The first major disaster happened in 116 AD, when the Roman emperor Trajan managed to conquer Mesopotamia, and looted Seleucia and Ctesiphon. However, the Romans were not able to hold the new province for long, and already the successor of Trajan,

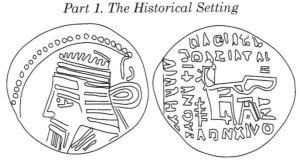

Fig. 7. Coin of Vologases I with Aramaic legend. The monogram indicates that the coin was minted in Ecbatana.

the emperor Hadrian, withdrew his troops from Mesopotamia. Nevertheless, the empire was certainly weakened. Mainly from different issues of coins, we learn that there were constantly usurpers in the empire, and in the east the mighty empire of Kushan now also threatened the Parthians.

Vologases IV (147/8-191/2 AD) reigned for over forty years. There are signs that he managed to re-establish Parthian power to a certain extent, but relations with the Romans remained critical, and war broke out once more between them. In 164/5 AD the emperor Lucius Verus invaded Mesopotamia, won several battles and looted the capital cities Seleucia and Ctesiphon once more. The Parthians retook most of their empire, but Mesopotamia was ravaged for the second time in 50 years. In this period, plague swept over the Roman empire, and must also have been devastating for Mesopotamia, although the sources report only on its impact on the Romans. In 198 AD the Roman emperor Septimius Severus managed to loot Ctesiphon for a third time, and occupied Seleucia. The Romans had to withdraw when food became short, but the whole episode must have contributed further to the weakening of the empire. The shaky state of the empire also seems to be reflected in the coinage of the period: Greek inscriptions are barely legible, and the figures turn into caricatures.

The final end of the Parthian empire came from a new quarter. Around 220 AD a new rebel kingdom in Fars (north-west Iran) managed to expel

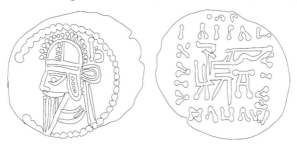

Fig. 8. Coin of Vologases VI with Aramaic legend. On the reverse is a seated man with a bow; in front of him is a monogram, indicating that the coin was minted in Ecbatana.

the Parthian king Vologases VI, and so destroy the empire. The rebel king, Ardashir, was the founder of a new era and new realm, the Sassanian empire.

Vassal kingdoms: I. Characene

The territory of the Parthian empire included several vassal kingdoms at various points in its history. Some of these, especially in the east of the empire, are often only names for us. Others are better known, because they minted coins, which have survived in numbers, and are recorded at greater length by classical authors. Characene is perhaps the best example. It was founded around 127 BC under Hyspaosines, and existed as an independent kingdom for a short period before being conquered by the Parthians. After the Parthian conquest it remained a semi-autonomous country with its own kings. It disappeared as a separate kingdom with the fall of the Parthian empire.

The kings of Characene are mainly known from their coins, consisting primarily of silver tetradrachms and bronze drachms with Greek and later Aramaic inscriptions. Down to the middle of the second century AD the coin inscriptions include dates of the Seleucid era, and these provide a secure framework for the chronological order of the rulers.[36]

Hyspaosines, also known as Aspasine or Spasines, was born in 209 BC and died in 124 BC. He was the first king of Characene, and its founding figure. Little is known of him beyond some references in Pliny, but he appears in cuneiform texts from Babylon, and issued his own coins. There is also a building inscription found in Bahrain, adding further information on his reign. Together these sources make him the best known king of Characene.

In the second century BC the Seleucid empire was in a state of disintegration. The Parthian king Mithridates I managed to defeat the Seleucid king Demetrius II Nicator and conquered Mesopotamia. Details of these events elude us, but the Parthian king seems to have kept the Seleucid administrative structures intact in the new conquered provinces, and even seems to have left old governors in place. Hyspaosines was one of them, ruling a province called Mesene, apparently identical with the 'satrapy of the Erythraean Sea'. After the death of Mithridates I, the extended Parthian empire was under threat. Initially his widow ruled as regent for their young son Phraates II. The Seleucids under Antiochus VII Eumenes took advantage of the situation to launch an attack on Mesopotamia, to reconquer the newly lost province. He was successful, and Mesopotamia became Seleucid again. However, the renewed Seleucid rule seems not to have been stable, as the few sources of the period report ongoing wars.

It was during this unstable period that Hyspaosines declared independence. His origins and power-base are unknown. Pliny the Elder mentions that he was the son of a certain 'king of the neighbouring Arabs'

Sagdodonacos; the name Hyspaosines itself may be a Greek version of the Iranian Vispa-chanah. From the cuneiform sources, it is possible to follow several military campaigns he conducted to take over parts of Mesopotamia and Persia. In 138 BC he conquered Elymais, the Persian province just east of his own territory. Several years later he seems to have ruled Babylon, and he is called 'king' for the first time on 24 June 127 BC. Three years later, in 124 BC, he fell ill and died, but coins with his name continued to be issued until 121 BC. The inscription found in Bahrain demonstrates that he also ruled this island, and gives the name of his queen: 'In the name of king Hyspaosines and queen Thalassia, Kephisodoros, governor of Tylos and the islands (dedicated) this temple to the Dioscuri Saviour-gods'.[37] Queen Thalassia also appears in the 'Astronomical Diaries' (see p. 97).

The Astronomical Diaries from Babylon inform us that after Hyspaosines' death, his wife Thalassia tried to install a young son on the throne. The name of this son is not known and it can only guessed whether he is identical with king Apodacus who appears on coins dated to the years 110/9-104/3 BC. If this is the case, a dynasty was established. The following king Tiraius I is also known only from coins, which are dated to the years 95/4-90/89 BC. Tiraius II is known from his coins dated to the years 79/8 to 49/8 BC, providing evidence for quite a long reign. This king is also mentioned by the Greek writer Lucian, who says that he was the third king after Hyspaosines and died in his 92nd year of life. King Artabazus I is so far known only from one coin dated to the year 49/8 BC. He may have been in power for only a brief time. A king with the same name is again mentioned by Lucian who said that he was installed as king at the age of 86, which seems to fit a king with a short reign. The coins of Attambelus I date between 47/6 and 25/4 BC. He was followed by Theonesius I whose reign can be dated 25/4 to 19/8 BC, and by Attambelus II who ruled from 17/6 BC to 8/9 AD. Coins of the latter have been found at several places, notably at Susa, on the island of Failaka and on the Kuwaitan islands al-'Akaz and Umm an-Namal, providing evidence for the wider trade in this period. This is no surprise, as we know from several inscriptions that Characene was an important trading land. Caravans arrived there from Syria, and the goods were transferred to ships headed for India.

The reign of Abinergaus I seems to have been interrupted, for unknown reasons. His first reign perhaps lasted for only a short period, as coins are known for only a few years (10/1-13/4). A gap of about ten years in the coinage follows. Into this gap must be placed the reign of a king Orabazes who is only known from an inscription found at Palmyra. The inscription is badly damaged, but can be dated to this time because it mentions Germanicus, nephew of the Roman emperor Tiberius, and Shamshigeram, king of Emesa. The inscription is the only attestation for Orabazes, besides being one of the first items of evidence for trade between Palmyra and Characene. At some point King Abinergaus I ascended the throne again.

His second reign is known from a single coin, dated to year 333 (22/3 AD). He is also mentioned by the Jewish writer Josephus as Abennerigus. Monobazus I, the king of Adiabene (in modern Syria) had sent his son and heir, Izates, to Charax Spasinou, where he converted to Judaism, providing evidence for a Jewish community in the city.

Attambelus III is known from coins dating from years 349 to 355 (37/8-44/5). Theonesius II is attested on only one coin which is datable to year 357 (46/7 AD), and can only have ruled for a short period. It is possible that he was followed by a king with the same name: Theonesius (III). Only one coin is known from this ruler, datable to year 363 (52/3 AD). However, the distinction between Theonesius II and III was based on the different style of the coins, and it is still possible that we are dealing with just one person. From this time onwards the kings of Characene no longer minted silver coins, perhaps indicating a loss of economic power. Another option is that the central Parthian government started to control the minting of coins to demonstrate their own power. According to the coins, Attambelus IV dates to 54/5-64/5 AD (365-375) and Attambelus V to 73/4 (384). After this group of meagrely attested kings there is a gap of almost 30 years for which no coins can be securely assigned to the kings of Characene. Presumably at this point the Parthians directly controlled the kingdom without placing a king there. The evidence for this comes from a later inscription. Of King Meredates, who reigned from *c.* 131 to 150 AD, we know that he was the son of the Parthian king Pacorus, who is mentioned in one inscription as ruler of Characene. Pacorus ruled from 77/8 to 108/9 AD, precisely within this gap in the numismatic evidence. We have no clue as to why the Parthian king should have suddenly chosen to exercise direct rule over Characene. Is it possible that the province had became too independent, or was there a revolt?

Coins minted by kings of Characene resume under king Attambelus VI. His coins are dated to the years 412-416 (101/2-105/6 AD). Some of them were found at ad-Dur in what is now the United Arabian Emirates, providing further evidence for international trade in the period. Theonesius IV is known from coins dated to the years 421-423 (110/1-112/3 AD). His successor was Attambelus VII, whose coins start in year 424 (113/4 AD). He is one of the few kings known from ancient histories. In these years the Roman emperor Trajan invaded Parthia, conquering its capital Ctesiphon and moving on to the Gulf, where he met the king of Characene. According to the Greek historian Cassius Dio, this local king was friendly to Trajan, although, despite his pro-Roman stance, he was required to pay tribute. Roman rule over Mesopotamia did not last long: Hadrian, Trajan's successor, evacuated the new province. An interesting feature of the coins from Characene is their Hellenistic style up to the second century AD. On coins from Characene, the bust of the king always faces right, as it does on Seleucid coins, whereas on Parthian coins the king faces left. The style of the depicted rulers remains strongly within Hellenistic traditions, while

Fig. 9. Coin of Meredates.

Parthian coins developed their own separate style in the first century BC. Charax Spasinou was a Greek foundation and one wonders whether the city stayed true for a longer time to its Hellenistic roots.

The next king, Meredates, is known from several sources. He was the son of the Parthian king Pacorus. It is again a mystery how he rose to the throne, and why he did not follow his father directly, but two other rulers. The earliest reference to Meredates is in an inscription found at Palmyra dated to year 442 (April 131 AD). It mentions the erection of a statue to honour a Palmyrenean trader called Yarhai by traders who lived in Charax Spasinou. The next evidence for Meredates comes from several coins dated to year 454 (143/4 AD). From the coins we learn that he was the 'son of Pacorus, King of Kings, King of the Omani'. Finally, Meredates is known from a statue found in Seleucia. On this statue of Heracles are two inscriptions, one in Greek, one in Parthian, essentially with the same text:

> In year 642 (151 AD) following the way of the Greeks, the King of Kings Arsaces Vologaises, son of king Meredates, went to war against Mesene, against king Meredates, son of Pacorus, who was king before him. After he expelled Meredates from the Mesene he became ruler of the whole of Mesene. This bronze statue of Heracles which he brought from the Mesene he dedicated to the temple of the god Apollo, who sits in front of the bronze gate.

The reason for this invasion and the expulsion of king Meredates remain unknown. Characene might have achieved independent status for a while under Meredates. On the other hand, during this period it might have become a vassal state of the Romans, rather than of the Parthians. However, this remains mere guesswork. In the following years, Characene probably returned to being part of the Parthian empire once more. There are coins of a king Orabazes II dated between 462 and 466 (151/2 to 155/6 AD). His coins bear Aramaic inscriptions next to the Greek, and are the last dated coins from Characene. From this time, the coins also became Parthian in style, with fewer and fewer Greek elements. Abinergaus II is only vaguely datable to the second century AD. Attambelus VIII appears on the coins of king Maga as his father – a small dynasty within the succession of kings. The last ruler is known only from the annals of Muhammad b. Garir at-Tabari who described in his account of the conquests of the first Sassanian king Ardashir I how he conquered the

Messene and killed king Bandu (in other versions: Bindoe or Bevda) in 224 or 226 AD. It has been assumed that this name is a garbled version of Abinergaus. King Ardashir I founded several new cities in the Characene, but the province lost its independence and was now part of the Sassanian empire. Ardashir I placed his son Mihr-Sah as governor of Characene.

Vassal kingdoms: II. Elymais

Elymais is the Greek name for a region in the south-west of modern Iran, on the borders of modern Iraq. In many respects it corresponds to the ancient state of Elam, one of the oldest known civilisations, with urban traditions going back to the fourth millennium BC. It has thus been proposed that Elymais is just the Greek version of the more ancient name Elam. However, the two toponyms seem not to be strictly identical. Susa was clearly the main city of the kingdom of Elam, but did not always belong to Elymais, whose capital was Seleucia on the Hedyphon, not yet securely located. According to Strabo, the region was divided into three provinces, called Gabiane, Massabatene and Korbiane.[38] In contrast, the region around Susa was named Susiana. However, the picture presented by classical Greek and Roman authors is not fully conclusive. In some sources they appear as separate provinces, in other sources Susiana is part of Elymais.[39] Elymais was a mountainous region, while Susiana was basically the wide fertile plain, heartland of the Elamite civilisation.

Elymais lies far removed from the Greek homeland and the Roman empire. Few events in the region involved the political affairs of the Mediterranean, and as a result the region is not often mentioned by classical authors.[40] The lack of classical sources makes the history of the region in Seleucid and Parthian times particularly difficult to reconstruct, and heavily reliant on coins issued by local kings. In addition some kings' names are known from monuments found in the region, but they are hard to bring into a wider picture, as many kings had identical names, and so undated inscriptions are almost impossible to assign to a particular ruler. Nevertheless, Elymais is of interest for several reasons. First of all, there is Susa, one of the most important cities of the Seleucid and Parthian empires. From excavations it is possible to gain some idea of the place in these periods. The city was home to a substantial Greek population, and there are signs that Susa kept its Greek administration and a general Greek character for a long time. Despite that, the overall appearance of the city during these centuries remains rather enigmatic. Furthermore, Elymais is an attractive subject for historians, precisely because its history is still so relatively unknown; apart from the coins, its kings do not appear in any of the inscriptions at Susa. Finally, there are many rock reliefs in Elymais. Their dating and interpretation remain much disputed, but they are still an important source for local Parthian art. Rock reliefs have a long tradition in the art of Elam and the Persian empire. In this region, they

Fig. 10. Rock statue of Heracles at Behistun.

are well attested under Achaemenid rule, and some examples might date back to the middle of the second millennium BC.[41] The rock sculpture of Heracles is dated by an inscription to 148 BC, right at the end of Seleucid rule in this region. According to the inscription the statue was carved for Hyacinthos, son of Pantauchos, in honour of Cleomenis, the local Seleucid governor.[42] The figure of Heracles is in a purely Hellenistic style, although its bold appearance does make it look somehow 'un-Greek'.

Many more rock reliefs are known from the following Parthian period. They provide an important guide to local art in the Parthian empire. In contrast to the Seleucid statue, these are often rather flat reliefs in typical Parthian style. People are most often shown in frontal depiction, with little interaction even in narrative scenes. The reliefs are often hard to date. There are inscriptions and even kings' names, but these are names that could refer to more than one king, and there are almost no year-datings.

Returning to the history of Elymais, it is first mentioned by a companion of Alexander the Great called Nearchus, who took the sea route from the Indus Valley back to Mesopotamia. His own account of the journey is not preserved, but it is cited by Strabo.[43] The Elymaeans are described as a plundering group of people in the neighbourhood of Susiana and the Persians. With the conquest of the Persian empire by Alexander the Great, Elymais became a province first of his realm and shortly afterwards of the

Fig. 11. Parthian rock relief at Hung-i Nauruzi.

Seleucid empire. The Seleucid province appears only rarely in classical sources. The next reference comes a century after its first appearance in Nearchus' account.

For the beginning of the reign of Antiochus III (223-187 BC), the historian Polybius reports that people of Elymais supported the revolt of a certain Molon, satrap of Media, who in turn attacked Diogenes, the satrap of the Susiana. Molon managed to gain power even over Mesopotamia, but his revolt was suppressed in 220 BC.[44] Towards the end of his reign, Antiochus III had lost important parts of the Seleucid empire to the Romans, and was being forced to pay a great deal of money to them. In 187 BC he attacked the temple of Bel in Elymais; short of money, he wanted to loot the treasury of the temple, which was obviously a rich institution. The plot failed and Antiochus III was killed by the local population. Under Antiochus IV (175-164 BC) we hear again that the Seleucid king invaded the province with the intention of looting a temple. This time it is the temple of Artemis, like that of Bel not yet securely located. The two events are strikingly similar, and some scholars have argued that ancient writers confused reports of a single episode. However, nowadays it is generally agreed that there was no confusion, and that these are two separate events.[45] If history really did repeat itself in this manner, it may reveal some underlying cultural misunderstanding between Greek Seleucid and

24

ancient Iranian and Mesopotamian attitudes to kingship and temples. For the Greeks, the temple treasury may have been regarded as the personal property of the king, who could then legitimately draw on its resources as necessary. In ancient Mesopotamian sources, temple treasuries belong to the gods, and it would be a heinous crime for a ruler to seize them.

In the years that followed, Seleucid rule became weaker and weaker in the east of their empire. Characene became independant; the same happened with Elymais.

The first ruler of Elymais may have been Kamnaskires, who also appears in Babylonian Astronomical Diaries. Kamnaskires certainly had great ambitions, and in Susa he replaced the Seleucid pretender to the throne, Alexander Balas. The Babylonian Diaries for the year 145 BC record that his troops marched on Babylon. He must be identical to the person known in Greek form as Kamnaskires Nikephoros on coins dated 147-140 BC.[46] In this period of constant struggle there seems to have been a common pattern of local rulers changing sides. In 140 BC Elymais supported the Seleucid king Demetrius II against the Parthians and perhaps against Characene under Hyspaosines. However, Elymais was defeated by Hyspaosines. This event is known from cuneiform texts, and might relate to an attack on Elymais by the Parthian king Mithridates I in the same years, in revenge for helping the Seleucids.

For the next years almost nothing is known about its history, but Elymais seems to have come under Parthian control as a semi-independent kingdom.

King Okkonapses[47] (c. 139 BC) is only known from four coins. Many more are preserved from Tigraios' reign (c. 138/7-133/2 BC). Most of the latter's coins were found in a hoard at Susa, but it is not certain that they were minted there or that Tigraios ruled from there.[48] The coins are purely Greek in style but the portrait of the king, shown in profile, is rather poorly modelled. On the reverse several motifs appear, such as Artemis, an eagle, a palm tree or the head of a boar.[49] It has been proposed that both Okkonapses and Tigraios were short reigning usurpers under the Parthians. After them, there are no coins attested for Elymais and no names of kings are known for the next 50 years. Perhaps governors ruled the province or the local vassal kings no longer had the right to mint coins.

This changed with Kamnaskires III, who is datable to 82/1 BC and appears on some coins together with his queen Anzaze. They are shown side by side in profile on the obverse. The king is depicted with a long beard and Iranian dress, giving his image a more Parthian appearance. The carving of the portraits is fine. On the reverse is shown Zeus, seated with a figure of Nike in one hand, and a spear in the other.[50] The prominent appearance of Anzaze on the coins of this queen might indicate joint rule by the couple, though her role is difficult to identify. She is called 'queen' on these coins, a term which could denote either 'wife of a king' or 'ruling

Fig. 12. Coin of Kamnaskires (III) shown with Anzaze.

queen'. Nevertheless, it was not common in any part of the Parthian empire for a wife of a ruler to appear next to her husband on coins. The other famous example is queen Musa, who was certainly a strong and influential person. Therefore, if Anzaze was not co-regent of Kamnaskires, she must have had some special status. Another option in interpretation would be that Anzaze was his mother, ruling for him when he was still a young child.[51] Kamnaskires III probably appears in the Astronomical Diaries from Babylon, which mention a military campaign of the Parthian king Orodes I against Kamnaskires (there referred to as Qabinaschkiri), most likely Kamnaskires III.[52] It seems that Elymais had tried to gain independence. This event may also be mentioned by Strabo, who briefly describes an attack by an unnamed Parthian king against wealthy temples in Elymais.[53]

The successor of Kamnaskires III was Kamnaskires IV, whose coins date to 62/1 or 59/8 BC and perhaps 36/5 BC, although the ruler appearing on the latter coins might be another king of the same name. One of these kings might be the ruler who had presents sent to the Roman general Pompey in the year 65 BC. Pompey was fighting wars in the area of modern Turkey. This might be a sign that the kings of Elymais looked for an alliance with the Romans against the Parthians. Together with the fact that Elymais minted its own coins, this might indeed signal that the kingdom operated at this time as an independent state.

Under Kamnaskires IV the coins show a decline in material and style. The earlier coins issued by the kings were tetradrachms and drachms made of silver. In the later period they were replaced by bronze issues. Furthermore, the portraits of the rulers were more stylised than before. While the earlier images of the kings often belong to the better works of Hellenistic portrait art, the later ones are often rather crude.

Although Seleucia on the Hedyphon was the capital of this kingdom, the kings often also controlled Susa and may have moved the capital there at certain times, for example after 75 AD. Here, we must bear in mind that in antiquity the concept and idea of a capital was certainly very different to ours. Government offices and institutions were far less important than nowadays. The capital of an ancient kingdom was often simply where the king resided, and that might change more swiftly.

From 75 AD onwards, a large number of Elymaite coins were deposited at Susa, strongly suggesting that the city became part of their realm. Already around 45 AD, under Vardanes I, the Parthian kings stopped minting coins in Susa, also a sign that the city and region became more independent.[54] In these years too, a new line of kings seems to have appeared in Elymais. This is indicated by the change of names. Kamnaskires was the most popular name in the first century BC. Now other names became popular. Its first king was Orodes, and another Kamnaskires Orodes (III), son of Orodes.

A third king in the new line was Phraates, son of Orodes, who was perhaps succeeded by Osroes/Chosroes. The coins of these kings have no year dating and bear Aramaic inscriptions. Here we see a general change known from other parts of the Parthian empire in the first century AD, in which Greek traditions were dropped and replaced by Iranian ones. One group of coins for a king with the name Orodes, maybe Orodes IV, is of particular note. They bear the bust of a woman with the name Ulfan on the other side. The placement of the bust of Ulfan on the reverse of the coins seems remarkable. On the coins of Kamnaskires III, Queen Anzaze was shown next to the king on the obverse. Ulfan might be the wife of Orodes IV, but this remains pure speculation. Orodes also appears in an inscription found at Palmyra dated 138 AD.[55] The inscription attests to trading contacts with the city and also helps to date the king, whose coins bear no year datings. The text from Palmyra is written in Greek, but there is also a Palmyrenean translation, much shorter and not so well preserved. Interestingly, in the Greek version Elymais is mentioned, while the Palmyrenean version names Susa instead. This might indicate that at this time the two toponyms were almost identical, at least for a writer in Palmyra, who doubtless had better knowledge of the region than Roman writers in Greece or Italy. Two further kings are known from a series of rock reliefs with inscriptions written in Aramaic, located at Tang-e Sarvak, a narrow upland valley of eastern Khuzestan: (A)Bar-Basi and Orodes. The latter might be identified with a king known from coins or the one from the Palmyrenean inscription, but the identification remains uncertain.[56] The relief shows the king lying on a *kline*, which was a luxury piece of furniture with legs in the shape of eagles. The king is resting his arm on a cushion. In front of him are sitting two men on a bench, behind him another one placing his arm on the king's shoulder. Several further kings with the name Orodes may have ruled in the second half of the second century AD. However, it is in the moment still problematic whether certain names refer to one or several kings.[57]

Finally, an inscription on a stela, maybe a tombstone, discovered at Susa and dated to 215 AD, attests that Khwasak was 'satrap of Susa' under Artabanus IV (the stela is dated 14 September 215 AD), the last king of Parthia. The stela shows the king giving Khwasak the ring of power,[58] most likely either confirming the position of Khwasak in Susa, or appointing him as satrap. This scene demonstrates that at the very end of the Parthian period, Elymais was again part of the empire. However, in 221 AD the Sassanian king Ardashir invaded Elymais, where a final king, perhaps called Orodes, had ruled.[59] Thereafter Elymais disappears as an independent political unit.

For most of this history, little is known of political life beyond the names of the rulers. Their real position within the Parthian empire is most of the time just guesswork. Yet a general pattern for both regions emerges from the distribution of sources, the style of coins, and the rare reliefs, inscriptions and mentions by classical authors. The reference to the gifts sent to the Roman general Pompey might indicate some kind of wish for political independence. Stylistically the coins of these rulers are much closer to those of the Parthian empire than those from Characene. In the latter, Hellenistic traditions are still visible in the first century AD, perhaps even in the second century. In Elymais these traditions had already disappeared by the first century AD, almost one hundred years earlier. We might speculate that that not many Greeks or Hellenised people lived outside Susa. The comparison of these regions allows us insight into the loosely federal character of the Parthian empire, and the different pace of change that resulted across its more independent vassal sub-kingdoms.

Part 2

The Places

The archaeology of the region

Mesopotamia and Elam are among the richest regions in the world for archaeological sites. Many of these have been at least partly excavated, but there are still literally hundreds of places which have never seen been investigated. Parthian sites do not attract excavators. Even at Charax Spasinou, the capital of the Parthian vassal kingdom Characene, there has never been any excavation. Therefore our knowledge of these cities remains severely limited. Better known are some of the more ancient Mesopotamian towns, which are of fundamental importance for Sumerian and Babylonian history. Here many archaeological missions have worked since the nineteenth century, and these have also uncovered remains from the Greek and Parthian periods, as cities such as Uruk and Babylon were still prominent centres then. Invariably, though, the main focus of these excavations has been the older levels, not the Greek and Parthian ones. Furthermore, the preservation conditions of the later remains vary. Qala'at al Bahrain, for example, is the main town on Bahrain. Its ancient name was Tylos. Many pottery sherds of the Greek and Parthian periods have been found there, but when parts of the town were excavated, little in the way of architectural remains of the period was unearthed. At Babylon much more was excavated, and here some Greek houses and even a Greek theatre were still quite well preserved. By contrast, the later Parthian houses were found so heavily disturbed it was not possible to reconstruct a single house plan. At Uruk the Parthian levels are better preserved; several plans of houses are known and there are many important finds from the period providing a vivid picture of life at the time. The best preserved examples of Greek and Parthian houses were found at Seleucia. This was one of the largest cities of the ancient world, and though we still have no clear idea of the city as a whole, many blocks of houses have been identified. These houses yielded not only numerous finds, but also good evidence for the development of material culture and domestic architecture. Susa is the last major city to be discussed. Several archaeological expeditions investigated the site, and they also excavated Greek and Parthian parts of the town. Little of the work has been published, however, leaving important gaps in our knowledge, at least at the time of writing.

Seleucia-Ctesiphon

Seleucia on the Tigris was the eastern capital of the Seleucid empire, though still well within its western half. The term 'eastern' simply refers to its position in comparison to Antioch on the Orontes, in Syria, close to the Mediterranean sea and therefore virtually at the westernmost point of the Seleucid empire. Another important city further east was the old Persian royal centre Ecbatana, mentioned by Strabo as a summer residence.[1] Seleucia on the Tigris was founded by Seleucus I around 300 BC as one of several royal residences, and soon developed into a conurbation of great importance. It was for a long time one of the largest urban centres in the east, rivalled in size only by Alexandria in Egypt and Antioch on the Orontes. It is possible that there was already an older town on the site, and that Seleucus I refounded it as his new capital, renaming and reshaping this older place. This kind of 'new' foundation is often visible in the Near East, and we will see the same thing happening around Seleucia when cities with new names were built just next to it. At about the same time as Seleucia was established, Ctesiphon on the other of the river Tigris was founded. However, initially Ctesiphon was relatively insignificant, perhaps no more than a suburb of Seleucia.

The city lay at the junction of two major trading routes, certainly one reason for its swiftly rising importance. One route lead from India, Bactria and north Iran, the other from south Iran, Susa and up to the Tigris. At Seleucia these routes crossed on their way on to Syria in the west and Anatolia and Armenia in the north. Seleucia was also connected to the so called 'royal canal' which connected the Euphrates with

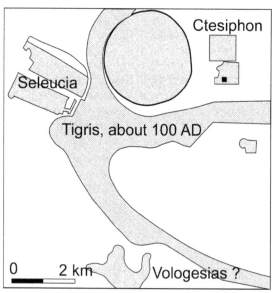

Fig. 13. Map of Seleucia and Ctesiphon (about 300 AD). The round city in the middle belongs to the Sassanidian period; the exact location of Ctesiphon is still under discussion.

the Tigris and was therefore one of the most important waterways in the region.[2]

Seleucia had the status of a Greek colony and seems to have been a vast city from the start. It is well known from ancient writers, although their information is often not easy to interpret. Some excavations have been carried out on the site, providing a very general impression of the place, although the picture is patchy and many public buildings of types known from other ancient Greek cities are not yet attested.

A canal divided the city into a northern part with palace and administrative buildings and a southern part with the houses of the population. A further canal divided it from north to south. Like most new foundations of the Hellenistic age, the city was laid out on an orthogonal street pattern, with blocks about 71 x 150 m in size. These are among the largest blocks of housing known from the ancient world. There were at least two theatres and one stoa is attested. According to Pliny the city had 600,000 inhabitants.[3] This number seems excessively high, considering the size of the city. The parts visible on the ground and located in test excavations show that it was large by ancient standards, but not on the scale of cities such as Alexandria, Rome or Antioch. Nevertheless, substantial parts of the town may not have been discovered or even recognised by archaeological surveys, leaving open the possibility that this high number is not far from the truth. Tacitus says that Seleucia had a senate of 300 people selected by wealth or intelligence, while the more common population had also some power, although he does not mention how. As long as both parties were united they were strong, and, especially under the Parthians, able to resist their king and his orders. The moment they had different opinions, the Parthians gained the upper hand and could seize control over the city.[4]

Many Greeks, Syrians, Jews and other people lived in Seleucia. It is recorded that the population of Babylon was moved to the new city.[5] In the end, the Greeks and Macedonians may have formed just a small proportion of the population, perhaps making up the ruling class. Little is known about the history of the city under the Seleucids. An inscription of Seleucus IV attests to the cult of Seleucid rulers. More information comes only from the point that the city became involved in several wars. We hear that in 141 BC the city was for the first time occupied by the Parthians under Mithridates I. In about 136/7 BC it was also conquered by Hyspaosines, the king of the Characene, perhaps only for a very short time. In 130-129 BC Antiochus VII managed to take it back, but from 128/7 BC Seleucia again belonged to the Parthian empire (Schuol 2000, 392). In this period of trouble, the city seems to have been devastated. In the northern quarter, next to the stoa, were found huge archives which had burned down at about this time. Some 36,000 seal impressions were found, preserved because of the fire. They must have once sealed papyrus or parchment documents, but these are totally lost. Most of the seal impressions are in

31

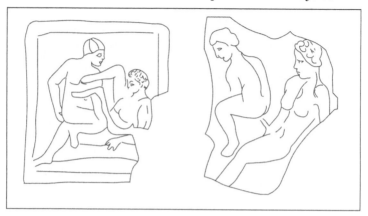

Fig. 14. Two reconstructed pinakes.

fully Greek style and many of them belong to the highest quality artworks of Greek glyptic, bearing the fine portraits of Seleucid kings and other important people. There were also several seals with obviously Achaemenid motifs, demonstrating that Persian traditions lived on even in the capital Seleucia.

In the same area a workshop which produced terracotta pictures (*pinakes*) with erotic scenes was excavated. None of these scenes were found complete, but they must have been quite popular as fragments of them were found all over the area.

Other parts of the city are not yet well excavated, or indeed excavated at all. The remains of two theatres have been found, but both are badly preserved. The same is true for several remains of temple buildings. It is not even possible to reconstruct their original plan or to say whether they were Greek or Parthian in style. Greek capitals were found, made of glazed tiles, revealing a mixture of Greek forms – the capital – and Mesopotamian technology – the glazing.

After the king of Characene, Hyspaosines, was expelled, the city remained under Parthian rule more or less till the end of their empire. However, ancient Greek and Roman writers always refer to the city as proud of its Greek origins, in their descriptions of the role of the city within the Parthian empire. According to these sources, the city was often in opposition to Parthian kings or even supported rival rulers. One example is the years around 35 AD, when the city declared itself independent. In the following years the Parthian king Artabanus II besieged Seleucia which surrendered voluntarily only in June 42, but was again attacked in 47 AD when the city did not support the Parthian rebel king Vardanes.[6] At about the same time we hear of Jews fleeing to Seleucia from persecution in Babylonia, hoping to find peace and protection in the great metropolis, after they felt unsafe in the countryside following their support of two rebels, which turned the local population against them (see p. 16). However, after five years Greeks and Syrians turned against the Jews, and Josephus reports that 50,000 were killed.[7]

Many Parthian kings are known only from the coins they struck in Seleucia, perhaps indicating that the city supported several rebel kings and was even their residence. Such is the case with Vologases (II) and Pacorus (II) in 77/8 AD. The coins of Vologases (II) are dated to the years 77-80 AD. At the same time Pacorus (II) was the legal king of the Parthian empire, but he also struck coins in the city. Vologases (II) disappears after 80 AD, and it seems most likely that he was defeated by Pacorus (II). The fact that Vologases (II) minted his coins in Seleucia might indicate that he operated from this city and was supported by its inhabitants, but was finally suppressed by the Parthian ruler. However, in the following years a certain Artabanus (III) struck coins in Seleucia, demonstrating that the city evidently supported another king. Artabanus (III) later minted coins in Ectabana, the old Persian capital, perhaps indicating that he moved his power base to another place.

In the second century AD the city was looted several times, and seems to have lost much of its importance. In 116 AD the Roman emperor Trajan took the city, and after it revolted it was looted and burned by the generals Erucius Clarus and Julius Alexander.[8] In 165 AD Lucius Verus repeated the sack of Seleucia, but spared neighbouring Ctesiphon, where he destroyed only the palace of Vologases.[9] Septimius Severus seized and destroyed Ctesiphon in spring 198 AD, taking a great part of the population captive; yet it survived this blow to flourish in later times, perhaps on account of the presence of the royal residence.[10] Seleucia is described as abandoned by the ancient writer Cassius Dio, and this the last time Seleucia is mentioned in ancient sources. In the Sassanian period some people seem still to have been living on the site and a huge watchtower was built over the former stoa, but the bulk of population had moved to the other side of the Tigris, to Ctesiphon.

As a leading Greek city Seleucia produced a number of outstanding writers and philosophers. Diogenes of Seleucia was a philosopher who was one of the main leaders of stoicism. His student Apollodorus of Seleucia (second century BC) wrote a celebrated book on physics. Seleucus of Seleucia is a well-known figure of ancient astronomy. He believed that the earth moved around the sun (and not the other way round), and is the only person known from antiquity to have followed Aristarchos of Samos who wrote a treatise on this theory.

The history of Ctesiphon is harder to follow. For a long time it seems to have been a suburb of Seleucia, lying just on the other side of the Tigris. The rival king Tiridates III (*c.* 35/6 AD) seems to have resided here and the Greek-Roman historian Ammianus Marcellinus (fourth century AD) mentioned that Vardanes (c. 38-45 AD) built its walls and made it his winter residence. There is no agreement on how far we can believe this information, but it seems clear that around 50 AD Ctesiphon was established as one of several residences of the Parthian kings. Seleucia and Ctesiphon seem to retain their independence from each other, but functioned in effect as a double city, and tended to share the same fate in the years that followed.#

Excavations in the 1930s revealed one of the blocks of Seleucia in the centre of the city. This block contains several house units and provides good evidence for the living conditions of the upper and perhaps lower classes in the city over several centuries. The houses are constructed of mudbricks. The walls are often quite thick and heavy, but it is not entirely certain whether there was a second storey. Some parts of the block are well preserved, others not, so that it is often problematic to distinguish units which belonged to single households. The excavators distinguished four main levels in the development of the city and of this block. The lowest (IV) dates perhaps from the foundation of the city to about 141 BC, when Seleucia was ruled by the Seleucids. Only small parts were excavated in this block of houses, not enough to provide a plan. This level may have ended with the Parthian conquest and destruction of the city. Level III dates from *c.* 141 BC to *c.* 43 AD, a period when the city was under Parthian rule but most likely still much under Greek cultural domination. The end of this level can perhaps be related to the siege of Seleucia and destruction by king Vardanes. Level II dates from *c.* 43 to 116 AD, and most likely ends with the conquest and destruction of the city by the Roman emperor Trajan. The last level (I) belongs to the time after Trajan, the end of the Parthian period. Finds of Sassanian objects indicate that the place was still inhabited after the Parthian period.

The block of houses consisted of perhaps six units of rich apartments. Next to the apartments, facing the streets, were found many shops. It is possible that these are the homes of the poorer population, living and working in the same small space.

A closer look at the houses found on each level and comparison with the next level provides evidence for the development of Greek to Parthian private architecture. In the lower levels the house units are arranged around an open courtyard, the Greek 'peristyle'. The larger house units seem to have had several, although it is not easy to separate them on the plan. Next to the peristyle was often found a large room of about the same size but possibly originally roofed. This is the location of the Greek dining room, or *andron*, and it can be assumed that it originally had the same function in these houses. The dining hall was certainly regarded as the most important room of the house, where guests were invited for dinner. This dining room developed over time into a typical Parthian architectural unit, the so-called *iwan*, which survived the Parthians and became very popular in Islamic architecture, especially in Persia and Central Asia. It is a large vaulted hall, open on one side towards an courtyard. It is an architectural unit which is not really on the outside, like a open courtyard, but at the same time not really inside the building, as one side is entirely exposed to an open courtyard.[11]

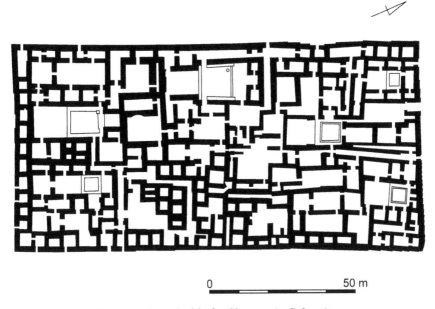

0 ————————————— 50 m

Fig. 15. Plan of a block of houses in Seleucia.

The peristyles and iwans were most likely decorated with columns. Walls were not painted, but several rooms had rich plaster decoration. This seems to be an important regional distinction. In the Mediterranean world, the houses of affluent people were adorned with wall paintings. Plaster is known from the so-called First Pompeian style, which was popular before 80 BC in Italy but also in Greece and Greek cities, for example in Delos or Priene, to name just two. Walls were adorned with plaster imitations of marble and stone blocks.[12] After that time, wall paintings replaced the plaster,[13] although plaster decorations also appear alongside. However, these later plaster decorations followed patterns of painted decorations. The plaster decorations found at Seleucia are different. They are purely ornamental, more similar to the First Pompeian style with little evidence that human figures played any major part in them. Perhaps the First Pompeian style was also used in the Seleucid empire. With the arrival of the Parthians, the Mediterranean and Parthian worlds developed in two different directions. In the Mediterranean, wall paintings replaced the plaster of the First Pompeian style, while in Mesopotamia the plaster decoration was developed further, becoming more elaborate, as can be seen from the evidence at Seleucia and other places. Although Seleucia saw itself as a Greek city, this evidence shows that in detail the Greeks in the Roman empire and those in the Parthian empire developed different traditions. Many fragments of statues of all sizes were found, demonstrating that at least some of the apartments were richly equipped with all

35

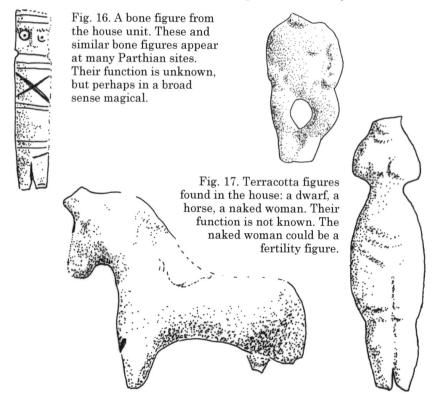

Fig. 16. A bone figure from the house unit. These and similar bone figures appear at many Parthian sites. Their function is unknown, but perhaps in a broad sense magical.

Fig. 17. Terracotta figures found in the house: a dwarf, a horse, a naked woman. Their function is not known. The naked woman could be a fertility figure.

manner of luxuries. However, there are hardly any of the marble life-size statues well known from many other Greek sites. Here again, the Greeks developed in a different direction.

As an example, one apartment in this block may be described in greater detail. This unit belongs to level II and is in the northwestern corner of the block. It dates to the first century AD, and may have been destroyed when the Roman emperor Trajan invaded Mesopotamia. It provides a view of a house shortly before this event. This was certainly the living place of an affluent family. The entrance, in the north, led to a small room richly decorated with plaster (1). The door itself was not preserved, and it is only possible to reconstruct it from other finds and from depictions in art. In Dura Europos in Syria many well-preserved wall paintings have been found, most often in the temples of the town. Dura Europos was on the border of the Roman empire but culturally belonged very much to the Parthian sphere. Therefore it seems certainly admissible to use the finds there to help us understand certain features not preserved in Seleucia.

The paintings in the synagogue of Dura Europos are especially well preserved. One of these depicts the temple of Solomon in Jerusalem. The temple architecture and people's dress are shown in Parthian style, not

Fig. 18. Representation of a door in a painting found at Dura Europos.

that of the time of Solomon a millennium before. The idea of recreating or reconstructing something of the past with its original appearance is a relatively recent trend, and not very common in the ancient world. Therefore these paintings inform us more about the Parthians at the time of the painting than about the early first millennium BC. Two buildings are shown, one of them with several identical doors. These doors have vaulted tops. Each door is clearly made of wood, as it is painted brown on a yellow background. It seems to have been made of several cross-beams forming squares. In the roundel above there are also cross-beams, here forming a semicircle. In general the door looks so modern that nobody would be surprised to see it in a modern city.

Behind the door in the house of Seleucia there was a small entrance hall (1). This room was richly decorated and would announce to any visitor that somebody of status and wealth lived here. On the ceiling of the entrance hall was a plaster rosette with a head in the middle, about 60 cm in diameter. The walls also had plaster decoration, in this case a meander-like pattern, perhaps forming a frieze along the top of the wall.

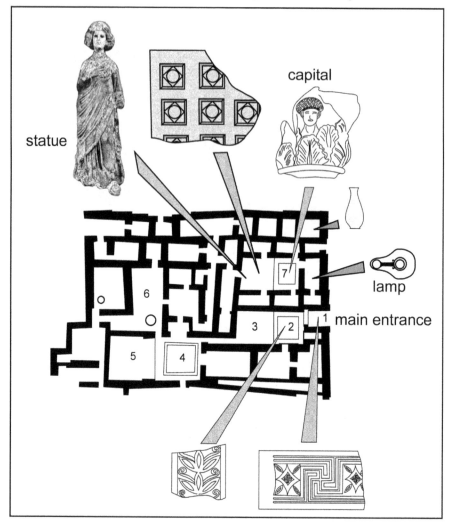

Fig. 19. House unit in the excavated insula of Seleucia with some of the finds:
the plaster decoration, a statue, a lamp and a vase.

The entrance hall led to a larger room which seems to have been decorated with columns and was perhaps a peristyle (2) with an open roof and perhaps with an iwan (3). There was again rich plaster decoration on the walls, showing that it still might have functioned as an entrance area to demonstrate the wealth and the taste of the house-owner.

This peristyle room led to another one, which was even bigger, and perhaps arranged in the same way with an open columned court (4) and a small hall, an iwan (5) next to it. From a visitor had to turn right, where there were the kitchen rooms with two wells (6) and also the entrance to

Fig. 20. Statue of a
woman found in the
house unit of Fig. 19.

the private quarters. The centre of the private quarters was again a
peristyle (7) decorated with columns and plaster on the wall and on the
ceiling. In this peristyle were also found several high quality statues,
further evidence for the high status of the owner living here. Most remarkable is the statue of a woman, about 56 cm high, made of various materials.
The face is of white stone with inlaid eyes, the rest of terracotta, painted
and even partly gilded. The statue is stylistically in the tradition of Greek
art and belongs to the finest examples known from the Parthian empire.
The figure may depict a goddess, perhaps for a small shrine in the centre
of the house, or it may have been a decoration for the main living quarters.
Perhaps it served both functions.[14]

Small figures made of clay are typical of Parthian sites, and indeed are
found throughout the ancient world. The function of these figures is not
always clear but it can be assumed that they had a range of different
purposes. This house unit too yielded many of these small images, varying

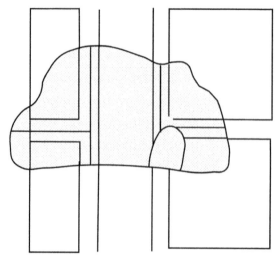

Fig. 21. Examples of the stucco decoration (partly reconstructed) with which many of the richer houses in Seleucia were richly decorated. Wall paintings have not yet been found, although they appear at other places.

considerably in quality. Figurines of naked women made of bone or terracotta were perhaps fertility figurines, intended to guarantee that the women of the house could safely give birth to many children. A figure of a woman holding a child might have had the same function. The statuettes of a dwarf and a horse are harder to explain but they may have been used in a specific ritual, or afforded a more general protective function. Some figures were found placed into or under the floor of the house, as if to protect it as benevolent spirits.

The function of the small rooms around the central peristyle (7) is basically unknown. From their scale and position, it can be assumed that some were bedrooms, as can be seen from parallels in the Greek and Roman world. Besides the figures mentioned above, pottery was found. There are a number of lamps.[15] In the kitchen area was found a nicely decorated pot cover for a vessel,[16] and in one of the side rooms of the inner peristyle (7) was found a glazed pilgrim flask.[17] Altogether, there are several hundreds different types of pottery vessels recorded from the excavation of Seleucia. Parthian pottery has often a thick green glaze and is therefore of quite distinguished appearance. Most often it is impossible to know the original function of single pots, but there are exceptions. Many small, finely produced vessels were perhaps perfume vases or containers for oils or other cosmetic liquids. Big vessels were used as storage jars and might have been used as containers for grain, fruits or other food. They are often found reused as water drains. Cooking pots are also easy to identify. These are large vessels with handles, often, not surprisingly, found burned. The rims are sometimes green glazed, but they are otherwise not very fine. Of rather modern appearance are several pottery forms which are almost closed with just

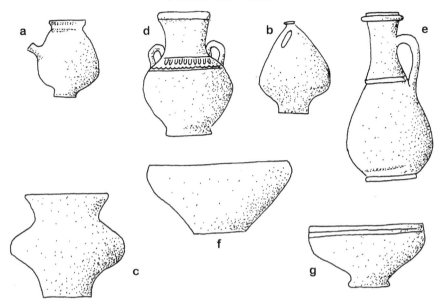

Fig. 22. A selection of vessels found at Seleucia. a: drinking vessel;
b: piggy bank; c: cosmetic vessel; d: green glazed vase; e: dark
blue glazed vase; f: bowl; g: white glazed bowl.

a small slit. These are ancient piggy banks: some of them still contained
their coins when excavated.

Other (published) finds are rare. There are some cosmetic objects,
notably bone pins. There were keys of a suitable scale to lock doors, and
others perhaps for securing boxes containing precious objects. For the
furniture in this house we have to look elsewhere.[18] It was mostly made of
wood and none has been preserved on this floodplain site, where organic
material could survive only in exceptional circumstances. Ancient houses
were sparsely furnished, especially compared to modern homes. Most
people, especially if not wealthy, doubtless just slept on the ground. Their
scant property was placed in baskets and pottery or sometimes into
wooden vessels, of which several examples were found at Uruk. Rich
people certainly had more furniture, but a house would most likely still
have looked quite 'empty' to us. Furniture can often be reconstructed only

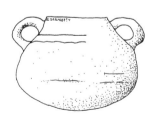

Fig. 23. Two types of cooking
pot found in Seleucia (left:
earlier, right: later type).
They are both green glazed.

41

from depictions in sculpture or in paintings. Few actual examples have been found. One exception for at least partly preserved furniture was found in a tomb not far from Uruk. In a burial chamber discovered under a great tumulus, four legs of a bed were excavated next to the skeleton of the dead person, most likely a high Greek official. The legs are made of metal and therefore survived. The rest of the bed must have been of wood, and has decayed. These beds were not only used for sleeping: they are equally well known as couches for reclining at dinner. This custom is well known from the Greek world, where the couch was called a *kline*, but also appears in pre-Hellenistic times in Mesopotamia, so in this respect the Greeks did not introduce a new custom. The Parthian couches probably looked similar to the Greek ones. There is plenty of evidence for these. In tomb reliefs from Palmyra the tomb-owner is most often shown reclining on such a couch, surrounded by his family.

One relief found at Tang-e Sarvak in the Elymais also shows a person lying on a couch. He is certainly the main person in the relief, and from the inscription might be identified as king Orodes (see p. 27).[19] Next to him sit two other men, maybe soldiers, also on a couch. The couch was certainly very much a symbol of status; only an important person had the right to lie on it, as can be seen from this relief. In the reliefs from Palmyra and other places most often the woman is sitting next to her husband, while he is lying, again indicating that lying on the *kline* was the right of higher status people, at least in art. Two types of legs for the *kline* can be distinguished. There are turned wooden legs, not preserved but known indirectly from several versions made of metal. The funerary couch from the Uruk tomb is one example of a metal 'turned' leg. Some Parthian paintings at Dura Europos and reliefs from other places show animal legs. On the relief at Tang-i Sarvak, the legs are in the form of eagles with spreading wings. Eagle legs belong to the later periods of Parthian history and are also attested for chairs.[20] The reliefs from Palmyra also show that these beds must have been covered with cushions and blankets. From the evidence in Palmyra it seems certain that these fabrics were richly decorated with geometrical or floral patterns.

Little can be deduced from the finds at Seleucia about the people's

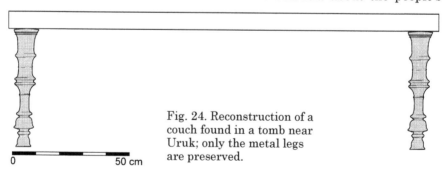

0   50 cm

Fig. 24. Reconstruction of a couch found in a tomb near Uruk; only the metal legs are preserved.

42

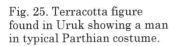

Fig. 25. Terracotta figure found in Uruk showing a man in typical Parthian costume.

clothing, and it is necessary to use material from other sites to reconstruct what they might have worn. Dura Europos in modern Syria remains to date the only site where larger numbers of textiles have been preserved, most of them probably belonging to the first half of the third century AD, during the period of Roman rule. The jewellery of the time has been recovered from excavations at many sites, but for the clothing we have to turn to other sources. Parthian costumes are depicted on coins, sculpture and wall paintings. These sources together provide a reasonably clear picture of the appearance of Parthians, though heavily biased towards the wealthy. Interestingly, women are always shown in Hellenistic costume, whereas men sometimes appear in a distinctive Parthian style of clothing, though they too can also be depicted wearing typical Hellenistic garments. It is hard to judge whether this reflects reality or whether there was also a typical Parthian style of dress for women not shown in art. The same question arises with Parthian men shown in Hellenistic clothes. Does this relate to reality or is it an artistic convention?

In the Parthian style, men wear trousers and a long-sleeved belted garment which varies in length, sometimes covering the knees, sometimes just reaching the hips. In basic outline this costume is known from the Achaemenid Persians, and arose from the requirements of nomadic life in central Asia. The trouser and jacket outfit would be ideal wear for riding horses, in stark contrast to the Mediterranean toga and tunic. All garments would hang loosely from the body, practical for the hot summers and offering protection against the sun, but also suitable for the cold winters when heavier fabrics were used but still in the same forms.

The wall paintings found at Dura Europos show that textiles had different colours, most often red, blue and green. At the sides there is often a band in a different colour. Additionally a jacket or tunic could be worn over this. In the second century AD the trousers and tunics are often richly decorated with floral ornaments. This can be seen most clearly on the sculptures found in Hatra and Palmyra. Neither place belonged to the

Parthian empire proper, but some statues found within the borders of the empire confirm this rich ornamentation of textiles as typically Parthian. A relief found at Bard-e Nechandeh (Iran, Elymais) shows a man with trousers and a garment over them. The trousers are decorated with a spiral pattern, while the over-garment shows several stripes decorated with spirals and geometrical patterns.[21] Another figure, found at Masjid-e Sulaiman, provides further evidence for the rich decoration of textiles. The statue shows a man in trousers and a tunic. On the front of the trousers there appears on each leg a line of spirals, a pattern repeated on the tunic. The rest of the trousers and tunic are decorated with a chessboard pattern.[22]

Men are most often shown bearded. The hair is depicted short but full, maybe indicating locks, with elaborate curls.[23] The attested headgear includes notably high hats, sometimes described in ancient literature, probably for comic effect, as the same height as a man.[24] A torque – a thick necklace-band – is often represented, which also made its first appearance in other, most often nomadic, tribes of Central Asia.

There is a certain trend towards luxury visible in these depictions, and some classical Greek and Roman authors also characterise Parthians in this way. For example, Plutarch provides the following account of a Parthian general whom he calls Surena:[25]

> Surena himself, however, was the tallest and fairest of them all, although his effeminate beauty did not well correspond to his reputation for bravery, but he was dressed more in the Median fashion, with painted face and parted hair, while the rest of the Parthians still wore their hair long and in bunches over their foreheads, in Scythian fashion, to make themselves look imposing.

Babylon

Before the arrival of the Greeks Babylon had long been one of the most important, if not the most important city in Mesopotamia. Its reputation as oriental city is (in)famous in classical Greek but also in Jewish literature and historiography. Persian rule was not popular among the inhabitants of the city, who therefore greeted Alexander the Great on his arrival.[26] He wished to make Babylon the capital of his empire,[27] and in a way Babylon achieved this status, if only for a very short period. Here he also stationed a garrison of Greek soldiers, and so from the beginning installed a certain number of Greeks in the city.

In 324 BC Alexander's closest friend, Hephaistion, died in Ecbatana, an important royal city in the west of Persia. His dead body was transported to Babylon and burnt there in a great fire which cost 10,000 talents. This was an enormous sum of money, testimony to Alexander's grief at the death of his best friend. Extraordinarily, the modern excavators of the site believed that they could identify the funeral pyre on its platform, easily recognisable by the red burned surface of the ground, although this

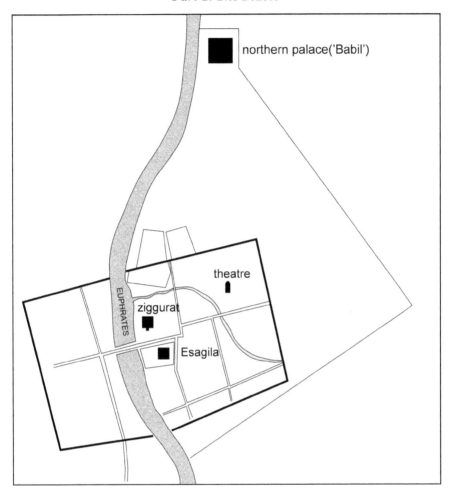

northern palace('Babil')

theatre

EUPHRATES

ziggurat

Esagila

Fig. 26. Map of Babylon.

identification has been challenged in recent research.[28] The funeral is described by classical authors. Alexander also ordered the renovation and rebuilding of the city's main temple, called Esagila, a complex around the temple of Marduk, principal god of the city.[29] Strabo reports that Alexander also intended to repair the Tower of Babylon and that 10,000 workmen were needed for two months just to remove the rubble.[30] However, the project never progressed beyond its initial phase, though the temple Esagila certainly continued in use for some hundred years. The rubble mounds left by this unfinished project were discovered by modern excavations of the north-east corner of the inner city,[31] and there are also cuneiform texts preserved, reporting renovation activities.[32] A mint was also set up in Babylon, although to what extent coins were minted is heavily disputed. Certainly belonging to Babylon are those coins struck with the name of Mazeus, who was the first governor of the city appointed by Alexander.[33] In a hoard at Babylon were found coins showing Alexander on one side, standing with Nike (Victory) crowning him, while on the other side he is depicted attacking two soldiers on an Indian war elephant, which may celebrate his victory over the Indian king.[34]

Alexander died in Babylon on 13 June 323 BC, at the age of just 32. In the following years the city was ruled by Perdiccas,[35] who looked after Arrhidaios (also known as Philip III Arrhidaeus[36]), a close member of Alexander's family and the most likely candidate for the succession. Perdiccas was murdered. The city saw political unrest and changed its ruler several times. Finally in 312 Seleucus I conquered Babylon. This event was regarded as a major turning point in his career, marked in later histories and by the king himself as the beginning of the Seleucid empire. After him, Alexander IV, son of Alexander and Roxane, ruled from 312 to 309. Although he was only young and was certainly guided by others, documents were dated under his reign. Alexander IV was assassinated along with his mother around 309 (the date is not certain). The real ruler was already Seleucus I.

Seleucus I did not choose Babylon as his capital but founded Seleucia on the Tigris, about 95 km to the north of Babylon.[37] The new city was more suitable for transport by ship,[38] and many people moved there, most likely from Bablyon. Antiochus I (281-261 BC) even forced the people of Babylon to make their homes in the new capital. From a reference by Pausanias, we might conclude that only certain people were moved, perhaps even only the Greek population.[39] At the same time the king ordered the renovation of Esagila, the main temple of the city, as we learn from a building inscription:

> After my heart drove me to build Esagila and Ezida, the tiles were formed with pure hands in the land Hatti, with the oil of the rustu tree. They were formed to lay the foundations of Esagila und Ezida. On the 20th Adar 43 (=287 BC) I laid the foundation of Ezida and the temple of Nebo of Borsippa.[40]

In 237 BC we have information that Seleucus II gave a great amount of land to several cities, including Babylon, Borsippa and Kutha. The temple district Esagila is even specially mentioned in the documents recording these gifts.[41] The temple certainly remained important in Seleucid times and many cuneiform tablets were found in Babylon dating to the Seleucid period and most likely belonging to a temple archive, demonstrating the active life of the priests there.

Around the mid-second century BC the Parthians took control over Mesopotamia. This happened for the first time shortly before 140 BC.[42] Their rule was not stable to start with, and Babylon seems to have changed its ruler several times within a short period. In 130-129 BC the city was ruled by Antiochus VII, the Seleucid king,[43] the city being his winter quarters on the way to conquer the lost eastern provinces of the Seleucid empire. For the years around 129 BC it is known that the Parthian king Phraates II appointed a certain Himerus as governor of the city. The king needed a reliable man to rule the Mesopotamian provinces, as he had to fight against attacking nomads in the east. However, Himerus appears not to have been a reliable governor and is mentioned by several classical authors as especially cruel. He even destroyed parts of the city, such as temples and the agora (the market place), and sold free people into slavery.[44] His rule can only have been brief, shortly after the king of the Characene ruled the city. In 126 BC offerings to the Parthian king are mentioned, showing that the place had again changed ruler. Only from 122 BC onwards was the city secure in Parthian hands.[45]

The Parthian king Mithridates II (*c.* 123-88 BC) established one of his residences in Babylon, demonstrating that the city was still quite important, at least ideologically. A Greek inscription from 120 BC mentions him. Another inscription dates to 109 BC and belongs to a certain Artemidoro reporting victories of 'ephebes' (young sportsmen) in the palaestra, providing evidence for a typical Greek institution even in Parthian times. In 52 BC Babylon was conquered in another civil war, by the Parthian king Orodes II. It is reported that traders of Palmyra had a branch office in Babylon in 24 AD; this is known from an inscription on the base of a column found at Palmyra. The column, originally supporting a statue in honour of a certain Maliko, was set up by the traders living in Babylon. According to the inscription, Maliko had provided financial support and help in building the temple of Bel.[46] All these references in ancient sources attest that the city was still a place of economic and political importance. We will see that there are remains from the Parthian period in the city. However, for the following years, ancient, most often Roman, writers consistently refer to Babylon as a deserted place, although there is evidence that the town still existed to some extent, maybe on a smaller scale. Livy mentions that the Greeks of Babylon had degenerated into Parthians. As the statement is very general, it might be doubted that he had any first-hand information on the city.[47] Another source of about the same mentions that the Jews were forced to leave the city as they were accused of poisoning the wells and causing a plague. This relates to records of the Jewish robbers Anilaios and Asianios, who looted and plundered the countryside around Babylon (see p. 16). Babylon is also mentioned several times in the Talmud as a local centre.[48] The Jews of the city and indeed of the whole region went to Seleucia, where they faced further problems. A Jewish presence is confirmed in the archaeological records of the city; there are several bowls with inscriptions in Hebrew.

The latest cuneiform texts from this place date to about 75 AD, when it was perhaps something like a middle-sized country town. Nevertheless, the renovation inscription for a Greek theatre is dated on stylistic grounds to the second half of the second century AD.[49]

Substantial parts of the city have been excavated and it is therefore one of the best places to follow the transition from a Persian-ruled Mesopotamian city to a Greek and then a Parthian town. The city of Babylon is one of the largest ancient cities, consisting of several zones. The inner city on the east side of the Euphrates was in ancient times protected by heavy walls. In the middle stood the main temple complex, named Esagila, with the temple of Marduk, main god of the city, and the ziggurat, one of the ancient wonders of the world. To the north, at the city wall, there was a huge palace complex, built for the most part under the neo-Babylonian king Nebuchadnezzar II (reigned c. 605-562 BC). On the west side of the river there were further areas of the city, also surrounded by heavy walls. An outer wall around the main city seems to have enclosed farmland rather than living quarters. About 1.5 km to the north, still within the outer city, there was another big palace complex. Smaller temples were everywhere within the inner city walls; some have been excavated, some are known from texts. Here too were living quarters, some of which have been excavated and comprise large houses of, most likely, wealthy people.

Babylon was known by writers as the centre of Chaldaean astrology and learning. The main temple of Babylon, dedicated to Marduk, functioned well into the Parthian period. Only small parts of this huge temple have been fully excavated, so there is little evidence for building activity or renovations in the Seleucid period. However, many cuneiform texts belonging to this and the Parthian period attest to a vibrant religious life. The temple is probably the source of a set of cuneiform tablets called the 'Astronomical Diaries'. These contain detailed records of astronomical observations and celestial phenomena. They start at the end of the eighth century BC and continue until at least 61/0 BC, well into the Parthian period. The diaries are of special importance as they also record historical events in detail. The astronomical content makes them a crucial historical source, although the tablets are often very damaged.

Cuneiform was therefore still known in the Parthian period; the last dated cuneiform text, also from Babylon, comes from as late as 75 AD. On other grounds several cuneiform texts, though lacking any specific year dating, may even date from the second century AD, indicating that at least some people were able to read and write that script. From the cuneiform texts we have some idea of the administration of the city. At the head of Babylon there was an official called 'shatammu', the chief administrator of the temple. With him operated a council of unknown size, and between them they ruled the temple Esagila, but also the city. There was also a royal official called the 'deputy of Nicanor', who acted together with the council and shatammu.[50] The latter was also some kind of local governor. Any type of Greek civil administration is so far not attested in sources from Babylon. However, this might relate to the type of sources that survive. The traditional Mesopotamian administration still used, at least to some extent, clay tablets. These have a good chance of survival in the archaeological record. However, the Greeks used papyrus and parchment, which has little chance of surviving 2,000 years. For the same reason, not much is known about the Parthian period, as the Parthians also wrote on organic material with little chance of survival. However, in the Parthian period a governor with the title 'pahatu' appears, also an important official, almost equal to a governor. The title itself is known from pre-Hellenistic times.[51]

Babylon doubtless changed little in appearance with the arrival of the new Greek rulers. The position can be compared to that of modern towns. A city built mainly in the nineteenth century still retains today, if not destroyed by war and rebuilt, the appearance of a city of that period. Only the surface details and additions, such as shops, electrical installations and cars would reveal that time has moved on. This seems true for Babylon and ancient settlements in general. The new era is only visible in archaeology from the small finds and certain additions to the old houses. The houses of the wealthy in Babylon were built of massive walls, which must have stood for long periods with no need to replace them after a short time with new buildings. Larger palaces seem to have been used without a break. In the main palace in the centre of the city, build in the neo-Babylonian period, around 600 BC, were found column bases which were added in the courtyards. Greek-style decorated roof tiles were found here as well.[52] The function of the palace in Seleucid times is unclear. It may still have had an official function, but it is also possible that less wealthy people occupied the building and that its rooms were divided into quarters for several families. This seems to have happened at least in Parthian times. Many burials of that period were found in the great courtyard of the palace.[53] The lower parts of two columns dating from the Parthian period were also found.[54]

In the north of Babylon there was an old palace building called Babil. It too was built in neo-Babylonian times by king Nebuchadnezzar. When excavated it was not very well preserved: only the huge foundation walls survived. The building might had have the function of some kind of summer residence. It was erected right next to the Euphrates on a hill overlooking the river. The building was certainly still used in Greek times. It may have been the residence of Alexander the Great while he was in Babylon, and perhaps the place where he died. The palace was most likely still used under the Seleucids and it seems possible that it was still an official building or even a palace for the Seleucid kings when they came to Babylon.

The archaeological evidence is quite strong for a further use of this palace. It seems clear that it kept in essence its old appearance in Seleucid times and only certain 'modern' elements were added. Again, several Greek-style roof tiles were found, which may indicate that courtyards were equipped with columns and Greek-style roofs. However, no columns were found anywhere in this building, so that is only a guess.[55] Perhaps the columns were made of wood and therefore disappeared and are no longer

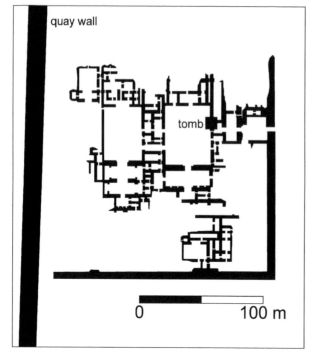

quay wall

tomb

0   100 m

Fig. 27. The northern palace in Babylon. Large parts of the building were destroyed by a fortress built on the site in later times, perhaps by the Sassanians.

Fig. 28. Roof tiles (acroteria) found at Babil, the northern palace in Babylon.

visible in the archaeological records. There are also fragments of wall paintings, indicating that a high standard of decoration was maintained for many years. The fragments indicate that large-scale humans were painted, as some fragments seem to show depictions of parts of dresses. Other fragments indicate ornaments. The technical quality is high. It was possible to observe five layers of plaster on which the paintings were finally executed.[56]

The building kept its importance under the Parthians and was heavily rebuilt.[57] Some of the paintings might even belong to this period. A large tomb with several chambers was installed under the floor in the middle of the palace. Compared with the hundreds of burials found in other places in the town, the tomb is impressive and it seems likely that local officials or a wealthy Parthian family living in Babylon was buried here. Altogether the palace provides the strong impression that an old building was maintained for a long time in and only parts were modernised. The Greeks might have kept it on purpose for its old style, as reference and in respect to the earlier Babylonians. It also must have provided some feeling of nostalgia to live in a building from which an extensive empire was once ruled.

A totally different case are buildings erected under the Greeks and in Greek style with functions unknown to the local Babylonians. The most impressive example of the new era and so far the only known new and fully excavated official building of the town, was a theatre with a palaestra alongside. The theatre was perhaps built under Alexander the Great or shortly afterwards.[58] It was situated in the northern part of the city, within the inner city wall, close to and partly built into the rubble heaps placed here after the renovations of the temples in the city centre (see p. 45). The theatre was made mainly of mudbrick with many parts in terracotta and gypsum as architectural decorations. Stone is not easily available in Mesopotamia. While theatres in Greece or other parts of the Greek world are normally made of stone, the most common local material in Babylon is mud. In general, the workmanship of the building is not of the highest standard.

The orchestra of the theatre was about 11 m wide. The semicircle for the audience had nine staircases and there was a central wider staircase, a feature unusual for Hellenistic theatres. Behind the theatre there was a big palaestra, more than 50 m wide and 60 m long. The courtyard in the middle measured 28 by 29 m. The courtyard was most likely adorned with columns, although little has survived.

In the years after its construction, the complex was renovated and altered several times. The original building was quite simple, with just the circle for the audience and a more or less monolithic building forming the *skene* (the background building behind the platform). In a second phase a raised platform in front of the skene was added. The skene was now decorated with Doric columns. Later the orchestra was raised at least two times. Interestingly, no roof tiles have been found. The skene was therefore most likely flat-roofed, as is typical of buildings in Mesopotamia and rather untypical of theatres in Greece. A Greek inscription found in the neighbourhood of the theatre may relate to the last renovation. The inscription is of special importance as it dates perhaps to the second century AD, providing evidence for Greek life in the last century of the Parthian period:

Dioscurides (son of [...])
the very beloved [...]
the theatre [...]
and skene (newly renovated)

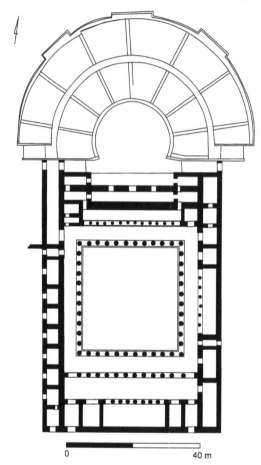

Fig. 29. Plan of the theatre and the palaestra in Babylon in the Parthian period.

0   40 m

Although it is reported in ancient writings that Babylon no longer existed in the second century AD, this inscription seems to prove the opposite.[59] The theatre may also be referred to on cuneiform tablets which refer to a building called 'bit tamarti' – 'house of observation'.[60]

Remains of another public building were excavated in the centre of the city, close to the main temple complex. These are the foundations of a colonnade flanking one of the main streets of the city, constructed under Parthian rule.[61] We know, from a list found in the city, that there must have been a gymnasium operating in the city, as *ephebes* and *neoi* (young men) are mentioned. Diodorus[62] mentioned that the city had a agora, not yet securely located. In the north of the city a further large public building of unknown function was excavated. The building was at least 140 m long and had several long corridor-like rooms. It is unknown when this complex was erected, but most of the finds belong to the Parthian period.[63] Furthermore, in the centre of the city a platform measuring 44 by 44 m was

Fig. 30. Fragments of gypsum found at the theatre in Babylon.

excavated. On the edges were columns made of burned bricks. The function of the building is unknown.[64]

The living quarters of the city are only partly known. Perhaps next to the Greek theatre there was a quarter of the town mainly for the Greek settlers, although this is not yet confirmed by archaeological excavations.[65] The centre of the Greek and Parthian city was perhaps still in the centre of the Babylonian one. Here were found the highest number of settlement remains and here also was found a colonnade of the Parthian period, something we do not normally expect to find in a suburb.

After the neo-Babylonian period the centre of the city was abandoned, but it was resettled with the coming of the new regime. The new people, certainly not only Greeks but people influenced by the new culture, moved into the old houses. Many of these were found in ruins, repaired and provided with new walls, sometimes rebuilt on the old ones. The climate in Mesopotamia is different to the climate in Greece. Houses are mainly built to protect against hot summers and cool winters. Thick mudbrick walls are therefore common and they are a good protection against the climate. It seems that not all buildings were renovated; several were left as ruins and perhaps used as gardens. Here were found wells, but also burials in Babylonian style.[66]

One example in the middle of Babylon is the large house labelled no. 1 by the excavators, built in the neo-Babylonian period. It was a substantial building almost 30 m long and more than 20 m wide. Its only

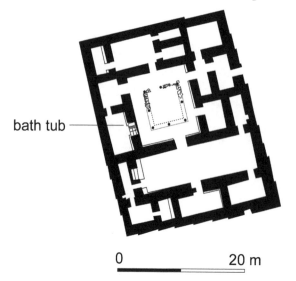

bath tub

Fig. 31. House in Babylon
with Seleucid-period
alterations (house no. 1).

0   20 m

entrance was on the east, leading into two smaller rooms behind which
was placed an open court. South of the court there was a spacious room,
perhaps the main reception room of the building. Around the court and the
reception were arranged several smaller rooms. After the neo-Babylonian
period the house was left empty for a while; one of the rooms even
contained a burial, made in the Persian period. Later, the house was
renovated: on the evidence of the pottery, this must have happened under
the Seleucids. The new inhabitants must have found it heavily damaged,
but most of the walls were still standing and therefore they could concentrate on repairing them, perhaps adding a new roof and some elements
which were regarded as necessary for 'modern' standards. Perhaps the
most interesting feature was the introduction of a peristyle, a courtyard
with columns.

Courtyards are typical both of Mediterranean houses and of houses in
Mesopotamia, but placing columns in them is characteristic of Greek
architecture. The columns in the Babylonian house did not survive, but
the bricks on which they were placed were still there. It can be assumed
that the columns were made of wood. Another new feature was the
introduction of a bathroom. One of the doors of the house was blocked
with a thin wall and a bath tub placed in the doorway. It is uncertain
how long the house was in use, but it is possible that people lived there
till the Parthian period.[67] Such distinctively new features were not
found in all houses. Typical finds of the period are Greek-style terracotta figures, known from many parts of the ancient world. Figures in
Babylonian style were found in great numbers in the lower levels. With
the arrival of the Greek era the style of many figures changed, though
old types were still produced.

Fig. 32. Greek-style terracotta figure, found at Babylon.

Fig. 33. Examples of Seleucid-period pottery from Babylon.

The development of the living quarters of Babylon in Parthian times is hard to follow.[68] The Parthian levels are among the highest and have therefore been much disturbed as they are most exposed to destruction by weather and later human activity. However, over the Seleucid levels which conformed heavily to the old Mesopotamian structures were found remains of later houses built on a totally different orientation. This gives the impression that the city, or at least the parts which were excavated, was abandoned for a while. When people came back they no longer cared about the old alignments of the houses and streets, but built in their own way. Little can be said about the new houses as they are so heavily destroyed. However, fragments of a painting, perhaps from a house shrine, demonstrate a certain level of luxury. The only partly preserved house was found near the old temple complex. This is where the colonnade was excavated and it therefore seems that this was the main part of the city in the Parthian period. The house is only partly preserved but in one phase had a peristyle with eight columns.[69] A remarkable find was a collection of objects of different materials, perhaps collected for making beads. These were cylinder seals and seals, eyes from statues and a sceptre made of onyx. The most amazing find is the imprint in asphalt of a wooden throne. The wood decayed long ago, but the asphalt on which the throne must have fallen survived. The imprint seems to come from the back of the throne. The legs were formed in the shape of a standing woman, holding a vessel in her hands. In the middle some kind of feather decoration is visible,

Fig. 34. Alabaster figure of a naked woman; such figures are typical of burials of the Parthian period in Babylon.

finely carved into the wood. At the top a fish appears, again finely carved into the wood. The head of a fantastic animal, perhaps a griffon, is also preserved, but the connection to the throne is unknown. Perhaps the animal was not part of the back, but from another side of the throne. Altogether, it seems that the objects come from the great temple or the old palace.[70]

To conclude, a word should be said about the cemeteries of Babylon. These were not placed outside the city, but within the living quarters. The dead were buried under the houses or at least in the ruins of deserted houses. This was already a custom before the Greeks arrived, and it continued under the Greeks and Parthians. There are three types of tombs. First of all, there are burials with clay coffins. These coffins have rounded ends and more or less flat lids. From the Seleucid period a sub-type is known consisting of human-shaped coffins made of clay. They show a face, a beard and long hair. These coffins are most likely influenced by contemporary Egyptian examples.[71] Their workmanship is most often rather poor and they are not really comparable to Egyptian anthropoid coffins, although Egyptian clay coffins are in general also most often rather simple. Secondly, there are small mudbrick chambers, just big enough for the body of the deceased. Only the larger ones can really be termed chambers. The roof is most often triangular. In a few cases remains of wooden coffins have been found. Finally, there are simple holes in the ground. These seem to be the most recent and are often quite richly equipped with pottery, glass vessels and jewellery.

Fig. 35. Babylonian sceptre.

Fig. 36. Paintings found in a
Parthian house.

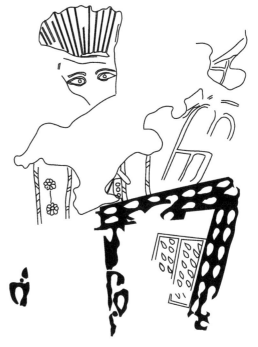

Fig. 37. Clay coffin
found at Babylon, the
human shape perhaps
influenced by Egyptian
prototypes.

Fig. 38. Alabaster
figure of a naked
woman; such
figures are typical
of burials of the
Parthian period in
Babylon.

The dead were normally laid on their backs with their arms at their sides, although the contracted position appears as well. Sometimes gold leaf was found on the faces of the deceased. Perhaps they were once covered with some kind of gilded mask.[72]

Uruk

Uruk (Greek: Orchoë) has a strong claim to be considered the oldest city in the world, and was already by the fourth millennium BC one of the largest cities of antiquity, on a scale and probably with a population to rival imperial Rome at its greatest extent over three thousand years later. In Hellenistic and Parthian times it was still an urban centre of considerable size. Old temples were renovated, new temples were built and everywhere across the city are signs of Greek and Parthian occupation levels, although little has been excavated of the living quarters from these later periods in its history. The Parthian and Sassanian levels lie closest to the surface, and it is therefore unsurprising that they are often not well preserved.

The city is situated in the middle of a region that has been extensively researched, with essential and detailed information available on a whole landscape with its small villages, towns and cities. The whole region was surveyed by archaeologists, who visited all archaeological sites and collected sherds and datable finds from the surface. Pot sherds are relatively accurately datable, so the distribution of sherds and finds from different periods makes it possible, without excavating every single site, to follow general settlement patterns in the area from the beginning of the Neolithic to modern times. A further result of the survey was the identification of canals. In common, probably, with the whole of Mesopotamia, the city and its environs were covered by a network of canals, dug to provide a reliable water supply for the fields, and certainly a prime reason for the agricultural richness of the country. The canals were also the most important communication routes.

According to the results of the survey, in the neo-Babylonian period (626-539 BC) the region around Uruk was already heavily resettled. Many new villages and small towns were founded or reoccupied. The causes of this local population boom are not clearly documented, but it has been assumed that it was connected with the general policy of the Babylonians of relocating captured peoples in other regions. The boom continued into the Seleucid period. Indeed there is almost no change visible between the Persian and the Greek periods. Evidently the Seleucid government maintained the structures they found in the countryside. With the beginning of the Parthian period a gap is suddenly visible, with a decline in settlement sites and prosperity. There are few finds from about 130 BC to the start of the first century AD, and researchers have not yet succeeded in explaining the change. However, in south Mesopotamia, the period witnessed the

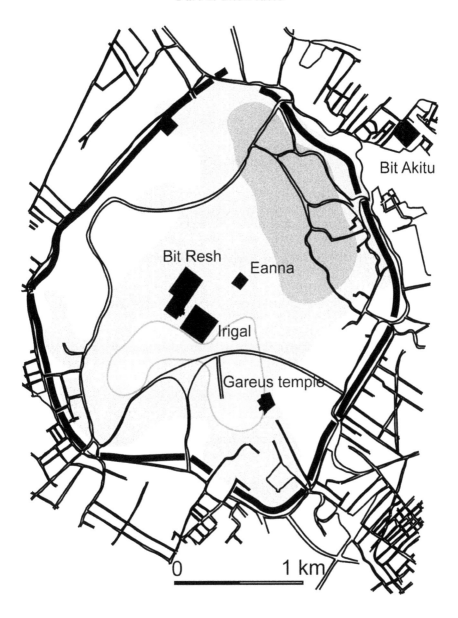

Fig. 39. Plan of Uruk in Seleucid and Parthian times, also
showing the elaborate canal system around the town
(dark grey = densely populated area).

emergence of the semi-independent kingdom Characene, centred on the city of Charax Spasinou, which had been founded under Alexander the Great in the fourth century BC. With the separate development of Characene, there was suddenly a new political and economic neighbour south of Uruk, and it seems possible that the new city and region flourished and attracted many people from the Uruk region.

The situation changed again radically in the first and second centuries AD. The region was again heavily resettled, to an extent not known before or after. Many new small towns were founded, some with impressive, perhaps public buildings. It has been calculated that the population grew roughly fivefold in comparison to the neo-Babylonian period. Most people seem to have lived in small towns, averaging about 7.7 hectares in area. Some 265 villages recorded in the survey were smaller than 4 hectares. It must be kept in mind that none of these Parthian villages have yet been excavated, making it hard to gain a clear picture of them. The settlements may have been less compact than in earlier times. Such a change in patterns of settlement, rather than population growth, could lie behind the immense scale of Parthian resettlement, or at least could be a contributing factor.

In the middle of the second century AD the boom came to an end, to be followed by a stark decline. Many places were abandoned or shrank in size.[73] This can be correlated closely with the political events and natural disasters recorded in written sources. It is known from ancient Greek and Roman writers of the age that the plague devastated their world. It is said that Roman soldiers brought the plague from the Parthian empire, providing direct evidence that the latter was also affected. There was repeated opportunity for contagion at this time, with the armies of the Romans moving far beyond the border zone, deep into Parthian territory, where they sacked Ctesiphon, the capital, and, under Trajan, even reached the Gulf.

The main source for the political history of Uruk is the corpus of thousands of cuneiform tablets, many found in official excavations with better documentation on precisely where they were unearthed. Most are administrative documents, written in cuneiform in Seleucid times. They provide detailed information on the social structure of the town, as also more generally on its history.

Unlike Babylon, Uruk did not lie in the political sightlines of the new rulers, so the earlier documents from this period bear few traces of the arrival of Greek rulers or Greek settlers. The first known documents after Alexander the Great date to the years 321-317 BC and belong to a priest called Iqisha; these make no mention of the new political situation.

However, other finds illustrate unmistakeably the arrival of new people. A little to the north of Uruk two tombs under a mound were excavated. In one of them was found the burial of a man lying on a funerary couch. His head was adorned with a golden circlet and the couch was a piece of

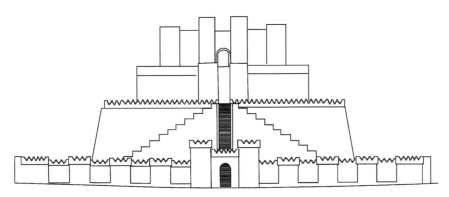

Fig. 40. Reconstruction of Eanna, the Seleucid ziggurat.

Greek-style furniture. Other objects found, such as the pottery, are early Hellenistic in style, and therefore belong to a period shortly after the Greeks had taken over. The whole ensemble is entirely un-Mesopotamian and specifically Greek in style, as if the person buried here was a Greek. For not only the material, but the burial customs too are foreign to southern Mesopotamia: although acculturated Mesopotamians might enjoy the material luxuries of their new Greek rulers, it seems less likely that they would adopt foreign religious practices so quickly. The rich equipment of the tomb points to a person of high status and one wonders whether this is the burial of a Greek governor, possibly even of the first governor of the region.

For the following years there is little direct evidence for the Greeks in Uruk. Perhaps in this period the canal network was excavated around the city, providing the fields with water and the city-dwellers with an easy and more up-to-date transport system.

The great period of Seleucid Uruk started in the middle of the third century BC. For several thousand years Uruk had not been a major political centre, but it had always remained a religious one. Its temples ranked among the most important in Mesopotamia. In the Seleucid period the city maintained this role, with renovation of old temples and construction of new ones. The chronology of this temple construction activity is still uncertain in detail. The greatest temple complex of Uruk was called Eanna, dedicated to the goddess Ishtar. However, under the Greeks it lost its pre-eminent position, although it was still used and renovated on a large scale. Under Greek rule, other temples became more important: the Anu-Antum temple; a complex for Ishtar, called Irigal in the documents; and a third complex, called Bit Akitu.

One cuneiform text dates to 321 BC and concerns Iqisha, the priest of Anu mentioned above, who was the son of a certain Ishtar-Shuma-eresh. In his text is mentioned for the first time a temple-complex called Bit Resh, situated in the middle of the town.[74] The size of the temple at this time is

61

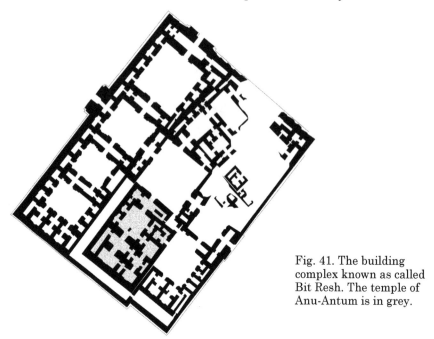

Fig. 41. The building complex known as called Bit Resh. The temple of Anu-Antum is in grey.

not known. However, building activity on a large scale seems to have started under Seleucus II. A local official, Anu-uballit Nicarchos, enlarged the temple complex and finished it in spring 244 BC.[75] It was 167 x 213 m in area and build of mudbricks. In some parts the walls are 6.2 m thick. This complex served not only as temple but also as administrative centre for Uruk. The tax adminstration of the city had its headquarters here. Among the numerous documents found are several mentioning transactions in selling and buying houses by officials working at the temple. From these documents we know that the temple owned land, and that officials had the right to live on it. Moreover they could sell the right to live on it, and they could have the option to buy it. These documentary sources make it possible to reconstruct the history of some families over several generations. In 201 BC a major addition to this temple complex was erected, the Anu-Antum temple. Measuring almost 53 by 75 m, this new temple was located within a spacious courtyard in the middle of the Bit Resh complex. Stamped bricks inscribed in Akkadian bear the name of Anu-uballit Kephalon, the governor of Uruk. The whole temple was again built in a purely Mesopotamian style without any Greek influence. The Anu-Antum temple was even decorated with coloured and painted glazed tiles otherwise best known from Babylon or Susa. They appear here for the last time in Mesopotamia. They are not of the highest quality. The preserved fragments show stars, lions and griffins. There was also a Greek inscription, which was quite small so perhaps not visible while standing in front

Fig. 42. Two seal impressions found at Uruk, one in a pure Greek style showing a woman, the other in a more Babylonian style; many clay tablets inscribed with cuneiform were sealed with them.

of the temple. The Anu-Antum temple was roofed with cedar wood imported from Syria. The complex is mentioned in texts as late as 134 BC, in the Parthian period. From texts it is possible to identify the names of certain parts of the building. One gate at the north-east of the building was called in Akkadian *ka-nakh*, 'the high gate', and here must have been placed a statue of the god Papsukhal, the protector of doors. It was partly gilded. At the gate called *ka-gal*, 'big gate', the fire god Nusku functioned as protector.[76]

At another temple complex called Irigal, dedicated to Ishtar, further buildings were added. This work was also carried out under Anu-uballit Kephalon, perhaps around 200 BC.[77] The amount of material used was gigantic: around 2.5 million mudbricks for the Anu-Antum temple and perhaps 5 million for Irigal. The latter complex covered an area of 195 x 203 m and was built in several phases. The double names of the two people involved in the temple buildings call for attention. They each have both a Babylonian and a Greek name, combining the old with the new.

The new building activity is perhaps connected with the military success of Antiochus III who pushed back the Parthians, the new power in the east. The king also conquered parts of the lands around the Gulf.[78] In these years the city seems to have had a economic boom and there is evidence that Greeks became integrated into the lives of the local population in Uruk. For example the governor Anu-uballit Kephalon, known as the great builder of the Bit Resh complex, married a Greek women named Antiochis. Whether this was a political decision to please the Seleucid kings remains unknown. However, unlike in Babylon, there are so far no signs of Greek-style buildings. It seems that at most only a few Greeks or Hellenised people lived in Uruk. Throughout the Seleucid period the place retained a fully Babylonian appearance. However, the region was of great economic importance, and under Alexander I Balas (150-146 BC) the city even had the right to mint coins, at least on a small scale.[79]

In the Parthian period the city lost some of its significance, but was still large, at about 2 square km, and was certainly more than a regional centre. Under the Sassanians, urban life continued at Uruk, but with a further decline in importance. The years after 141 BC were a period of many wars in Mesopotamia; Uruk seems to have changed its rulers several times. In 141 BC it was taken by the Parthians, and shortly afterwards Hyspaosines of Characene seems to have seized it. Only after 122 BC under the strong rule of Mithridates II did the situation stabilise, with Uruk now a permanent part of the Parthian empire. It has been assumed that in the troubles around 141 BC, when the Parthians attacked the town, the temples were destroyed. However, there is evidence that they were still in use to 108 BC, and they might have been burned in 87 BC, when Gotarzes I, a usurper, ruled in Babylonia. From about the time of Gotarzes I the remains of a wall are known connecting two of the Uruk temple complexes, the Bit Resh and the Irigal. This indicates that the temples were heavily fortified. As monumental buildings they certainly offered perfect strongholds.[80] At one point the temples burnt down, never to be renovated. Evidently at this point the Parthians obviously broke with the ancient traditions. The temples were now turned into residential areas, leaving only one small chapel in Parthian style built into one of the former complex walls.

The last major temple building project known to us in Uruk dates to around AD 65.[81] The temple was erected in Parthian style and is, indeed, one of the best-known Parthian temples. It was situated southwest of the old Mesopotamian-style temples. Within a fort-like enclosure stood the temple proper, fronted by a row of six Ionic columns. Behind this colonnade was a building of modest size, 10.7 x 13.7 m, made of burned bricks. Today the walls still stand to a height of some 4.7 m. The temple was decorated with arcades. There were also friezes showing fantastic animals in a more Greek style. Finds in the temple include a fine bronze lamp and the feet of a bronze statue, as well as remains of a limestone statue, demonstrating that the building was once adorned with sculpture. The stone figure depicts a person with shoulder-length hair, wearing a belted dress, and facing directly ahead.[82] This statue is roughly carved with emphasis on rounded rectangular volumes, without details and slightly out of proportion; by contrast, the bronze feet are naturalistically rendered in elaborate sandals. Of a third limestone statue only a hand with a bowl has been found. This may have been the image of a worshipper, placed in the temple, whereas the bronze feet may belong to a cult image in the temple.

The limestone statue could be much older than the temple, possibly even Sumerian in date. This is also known from other places. Notably, several statues of the Sumerian ruler Gudea were found in a Parthian palace at Girsu.[83] The temple in Uruk may have been dedicated to an otherwise unknown god called Gareus, as a stela in Greek with a dedication inscription to this god was found nearby. According to the text, the temple was built by *to koinon ton Dollamenon*, 'the community of the Dollamenes', perhaps from the region Dolomene, mentioned by Strabo as located near Nineveh, to the north.[84]

The only other temple building of Parthian times was found within the

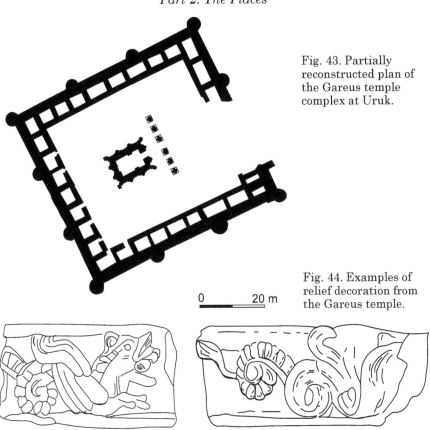

Fig. 43. Partially reconstructed plan of the Gareus temple complex at Uruk.

0   20 m

Fig. 44. Examples of relief decoration from the Gareus temple.

Bit Resh complex. Here the small chapel mentioned above was erected at the south-east outer wall of the old Anu-Antum temple. It consisted of just one room and was adorned on the outside with blind arcades. Another building of the Parthian period excavated at Uruk comprises a hall, almost 20 x 10 m, with an apse, an architectural feature that is rarely found in Mesopotamia.[85] The function of the building is not known, and might have been either religious or for official ceremonies.

In the temple complex assigned to Gareus were found several fragments of statues. However, extraordinarily few examples of Parthian sculpure are known, especially considering that the Parthian empire lasted more than 400 years, and was one of the largest empires of its time. The highest number of Parthian sculptures are from Hatra and Dura Europos, well-preserved and well-excavated towns in northern Iraq and Syria. Hatra was ruled by its own line of kings, who stated that they were Arabs. In this town the local upper class placed statues of their own in the temples. Whether Hatra was part of the Parthian empire is not entirely certain, but the art of the city belonged in a broad sense to the Parthian cultural

65

sphere. Hatran images show the strong frontality typical of Parthian art in the first and second centuries AD.

Two reasons may be put forward to explain the lack of large-scale sculpture at most Parthian sites. First of all, stone was not easily available in Mesopotamia. Many monumental statues in this region may have been made of bronze or even wood. Some Parthian bronze statues are known and indeed display a high quality of sculpture modelling, but most were doubtless melted down and recycled in antiquity. Wood does not have a high chance of survival in the archaeological record of the region. At most sites such statues would certainly have been lost, if they ever existed. However, at Dura Europos wood preservation is not so poor, and there are still almost no wooden sculptures. It might be argued that there were originally more stone statues, but that most of them were burnt for lime given the stone shortage in Mesopotamia. Any stone statues would have been an easy target, especially after the Parthian period when new rulers arrived and the old statues were no longer of any significance. Indeed we know from inscriptions found at Palmyra that many statues were placed in Parthian cities, at least in those with a Palmyrenean presence.[86] Another option is that statues were in fact not as common as in the Greek and Roman world. The examples found at Hatra might relate to different traditions of this town. Interestingly, at Dura Europos, a place under Parthian rule for a long time, and at least in part well excavated, more than 200 pieces of sculpture were found, but most of them considerably inferior in quality to those found at Hatra. The comparison is not exact, as Dura Europos statuary tends to show gods, whereas at Hatra many statues of wealthy and royal individuals are preserved.[87] In the final analysis, one wonders whether sculpture was simply not an important branch of artistic expression for the Parthians. This correlates with the Mesopotamian traditions of the second and first millennia BC, from which not many sculptures are known. It was obviously not an important art form in the region. Here, the Parthians, or perhaps the people under Parthian rule, followed local traditions instead of adopting the Greek tradition in which sculpture in the round was so important.

While the public buildings of Uruk are quite well researched, much less is known about the private houses of the time, as little has been excavated. From the beginning of the period come the remains of a house, quite closely datable because cuneiform tablets were found in it. They belong to the Anu priest Iqisha. The texts cover the period between the years 321 and 317 BC. Only part of the structure is preserved and excavated, but it seems to belong to a type of house with a central courtyard, as known from many other Mesopotamian sites and already attested some 3,000 years earlier. In the courtyard of this house were found storage installations. Around the court were arranged several rooms, in one of which most of the cuneiform texts were found, evidently some kind of private archive.

Fig. 45. Reconstructed plan of the house of Iqisha at Uruk, about 300 BC. Only the black parts are preserved.

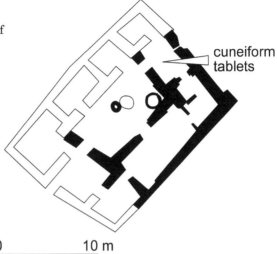

cuneiform tablets

Fig. 46. Nineteenth-century drawing of the ruins of a Parthian house in Uruk.

0   10 m

The architecture and style of the house are entirely within age-old Mesopotamian traditions.

The next example of a better preserved house in Uruk dates about 300 years later, to the Parthian period: the excavators assigned it the number U XVIII. Its plan and decoration clearly demonstrate that the times had changed. Unlike Seleucia, Uruk was not a planned town. The houses so far excavated seem not to have been laid out to a co-ordinated plan, but are

67

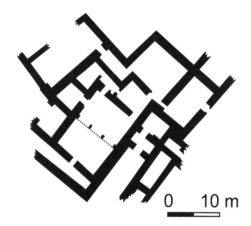

Fig. 47. Reconstructed plan of parts
of a house excavated in Uruk.

0   10 m

aligned more according to still-standing older buildings of the ancient city
with irregular street patterns. The remains of house U XVIII therefore
make a rather confusing impression, compounded by the fact that the
building is only partly excavated and not well preserved. However, it
still offers a general idea of a Parthian house belonging to a person or
family of high standing. The main feature is a courtyard with a hall
leading from it. This hall was perhaps a vaulted iwan, which is generally the most richly decorated room in a house of the period. This is
especially clearly visible here, for in this hall numerous fragments of
the original rich plaster decoration were found. In Parthian architecture plaster is often a feature of interior decoration because it is rather
soft and therefore not suitable for outside walls, where more solid materials such as terracotta were used.

Although in this case the decoration is much destroyed, with only small

Fig. 48. Examples
of wall plaster
fragments found
in the house
excavated at Uruk.

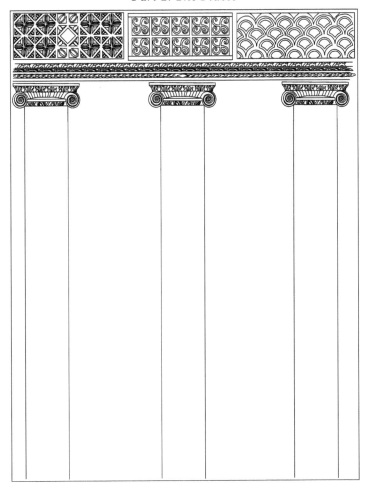

Fig. 49. Reconstruction of a wall in the Parthian house in Uruk.

fragments recovered, at least four types can be distinguished. (1) Fragments of flat painted plaster provide the evidence that the walls of the room had some overall painted decoration, in which plant motifs dominated. (2) There are many fragments of half-columns; it seems that the walls were divided by these into several sections. The smaller columns are fluted, the larger plain, both with capitals, belonging mostly to the Ionic order of Greek art, though one capital is adorned with a bust. (3) Numerous fragments with sunk relief decorative patterns were perhaps all placed over the columns as architraves, as can be seem from better-preserved examples. (4) Finally there are pieces from friezes of figures. From the size of the figures, there must have been at least two separate friezes. Altogether the fragments demonstrate the luxury and high standard of living in an affluent house in Parthian period Uruk.

69

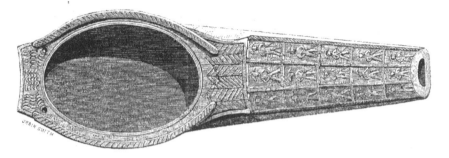

Fig. 50. Terracotta coffin found in Uruk.

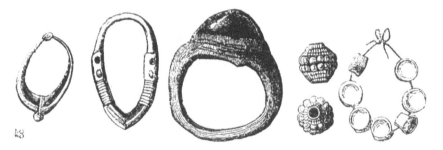

Fig. 51. Examples of jewellery found in Parthian graves in Uruk.

At this time, many living quarters, perhaps mostly for poorer people, were built into the still high-standing walls of the Seleucid temple complexes. Many of the old temple rooms were now sub-divided, and in the courtyards whole houses were even erected. One of these was a two-storey house with one room on each floor. It had a gable roof and terracotta cornices with lion-head water-spouts. The finds, such as loomweights, storage jars and household ware, confirm the impression that these were now residential areas.[88] Another well-preserved example was found built into one of the corners of the old courtyard of the main entrance gate. Here two walls were errected forming a cross and therefore four rooms. The outer walls of the house were the walls of the temple. In one of the front rooms a well was dug; there may have been an oven next to it.[89]

As in most Parthian cities, the deceased were buried within the settlement area, and the typical terracotta coffins decorated with stylised figures have been found everywhere. Some of the deceased, most likely women, were richly adorned with jewellery; exceptionally, the face was covered with thin gold leaf.[90]

Susa

Like Uruk, Susa is one of the most ancient cities in the Gulf area. It is located within a fertile region, and is crossed by major trade routes connecting India with Mesopotamia, and north Iran with the sea to the south, contributing to its political as well as its economic importance. It was already a significant centre by 4000 BC, and from early times was the capital of the state that we generally refer to as the kingdom of Elam. Elam itself disappeared as an independent state with the Assyrian conquest around 644 BC, although a succession of minor kingdoms seems to have existed between then and the arrival of the Persians in 539 BC. Under Achaemenid rule Susa became one of the capitals of their empire. A huge palace of the period was constructed in the north of the city. Its buildings were richly decorated with colourful glazed tiles and impressive columns, and it must have once been an extraordinary edifice, perhaps even the prototype for the later Iranian palace buildings at sites such as the better-preserved Persepolis.

Alexander the Great intended to make Susa one of the capitals of his empire. Here he celebrated a mass wedding between his Greek soldiers and Persian noblewomen – according to ancient sources involving no fewer than 10,000 Greeks. Alexander himself married two Persian women.

In the first years after Alexander's death a certain Antigonus was appointed satrap of the region and ruled there until 301 BC when Seleucus I took full control of Susa and the province. Around 300 BC Seleucus started to mint coins in the city. It evidently became a Greek colony, with the name Seleucia on the Eulaios. It is not known how many Greeks moved to the city, whether just some hundreds or several thousand. Greek names appear in inscriptions found there, but these might be Persians with Greek names who in daily life spoke not Greek but Elamite or another language. Nevertheless in official inscriptions Greek became the dominant language, as it continued to be into the Parthian period. Indeed, Susa is the place with the highest concentration of Greek inscriptions east of Syria. Only from the very end of that period is there a stela with an inscription in Parthian. Especially in the Seleucid period the city flourished as a trading centre. However, under Antiochus III the city seems to have lost this role,

Fig. 52. Symbol attributed
to the mint in Susa.

71

perhaps because the king founded Antioch on the Tigris, which then became the major port for the trade between India, Mesopotamia and Syria. Nevertheless, Susa remained an affluent city, most likely because of the fertile agricultural region around it. This is confirmed by the description of Strabo,[91] who states that 'Susis' was very rich in barley and wheat. He also mentions grapes for the local production of wine. Diodorus Siculus[92] mentions instead that the region produced rice, sesame and dates. An inscription from Palmyra may indicate that there was a Palmyrenean colony of merchants in Susa. The inscription mentions 'Susa' and 'Worod' (Orodes), the name of several Elymaean kings.[93]

There is strong evidence that the city grew considerably under the Parthians, a clear reflection of its wealth and prosperity. Large richly adorned houses were built, and there are also many well-built barrel-vaulted brick tombs in an area called the 'Parthian necropolis' in the eastern part of the city. From 138 BC to about 50 AD, Parthian kings struck coins in Susa, demonstrating that the city was regarded as a leading royal city. A large stela dated 21 AD bears a decree written in Greek issued by Artabanos II for two local administrators confirming a local election. The local officials hold the Greek title 'archon', providing evidence for a Greek-style administration of the city.

After 50 AD the Parthian mint of Susa ceased issuing coins, but several years later, around 70-75 AD, Elymaean coins were produced here. Evidently the city was no longer under full Parthian control. We know very little about the relations between the Parthians and Elymaeans. The latter were most likely vassals, so that the city was still Parthian, but with a 'local' king, no longer under the direct orders of the Parthian ruler. In 116 AD Susa received the Roman emperor Trajan on his Parthian campaign, the most eastern point a Roman emperor ever reached. Trajan stayed only a very short time, and his successor Hadrian soon had to withdraw his troops from the Parthian empire. The last monument of a Parthian king from Susa is a stela. It shows a seated and a standing man, each grasping a ring. The Parthian inscription over them reads: 'Artabanu, the king of kings, son of Vologases, the king of kings, built this monument which is that of Khwasak, satrap of Susa'. The stela is dated 14 September 215 and shows that Susa was again under direct Parthian rule. The function of the monument is unknown, though it has been proposed that it was a tomb stela. The language chosen for the inscription is no longer Greek. Very shortly after, the city was taken over by the Sassanians.[94]

The archaeology of Susa has a difficult history. The remains of the city cover an area of more than 80 hectares. Excavations started early, but under directors most interested in the earlier periods. The upper levels were simply removed to reach the lower, more ancient ones. As a result, any architecture from later periods was destroyed without being documented, and only some beautiful objects were collected.[95] In contrast to Babylon or Uruk, no great Seleucid or Parthian temples have yet been

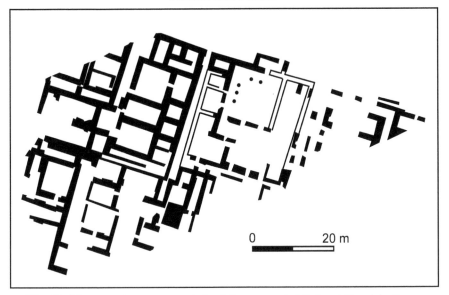

Fig. 53. Plan, partly reconstructed, of the excavated Seleucid level in Susa.

recorded at Susa, most probably because they were not recognised in the early excavations. In former times the main temple of the city was the one dedicated to the god Inshushinak. Whether it survived into the Seleucid and Parthian eras is not certain. However, from Uruk comes a text dating to Seleucid times, reporting that a priest from Uruk went to the land of Elam to research cuneiform tablets, copied them and brought the copies to Uruk. Evidently cuneiform was still used and known, and it seems highly likely that these old texts were stored at a prominent temple in Susa.[96]

Despite the lack of attention by earlier archaeologists, more recently some parts of the Greek and Parthian city have been excavated, correcting the gap in information at least to some extent. Although few public buildings from the Seleucid and Parthian periods are known, a number of private houses are relatively well preserved, making it possible to follow the development of at least one part of the city over several centuries. In the quarter of Susa called by modern researchers the 'royal city' an area of about 100 x 50 m was uncovered. Several levels down to the early history of Susa were exposed, providing a unique insight into the development of urban life there over several thousand years.

The houses on almost all levels were quite large. They were built of mudbricks with heavy walls, most often more than a metre thick. This part of the city was clearly always a quarter were affluent people lived. Level VII dates to the Seleucid period, levels VI and V to the Parthian period.

The walls of all the Seleucid period houses have been considerably destroyed by later Parthian building activity, so that no plan is complete; it remains unknown where the doors of the houses were. It is therefore

73

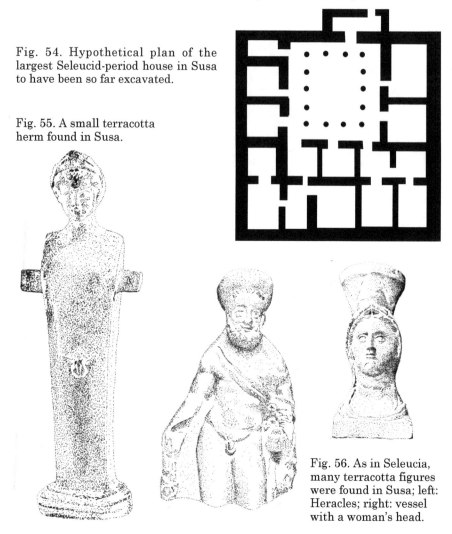

Fig. 54. Hypothetical plan of the largest Seleucid-period house in Susa to have been so far excavated.

Fig. 55. A small terracotta herm found in Susa.

Fig. 56. As in Seleucia, many terracotta figures were found in Susa; left: Heracles; right: vessel with a woman's head.

possible to provide only a reconstructed plan. In the middle of the exca-vated area there is a big house, about 25 x 25 m in area, with a peristyle or columned courtyard and rooms arranged around it. At about 10 x 10 m, the courtyard is quite large in proportion to the overall house area. The houses of this period also had bathrooms, and the finds include fragments of Greek architecture such as acroteria (cf. Fig. 28). All the houses are in a strict line, and one wonders whether the Greek city was planned in a chessboard pattern like the capital Seleucia on the Tigris. The bulk of the surviving area comes from one block of housing with the main entrances in the north, while the entrances to the more incompletely excavated houses to the south would have been on the other side of the block, facing

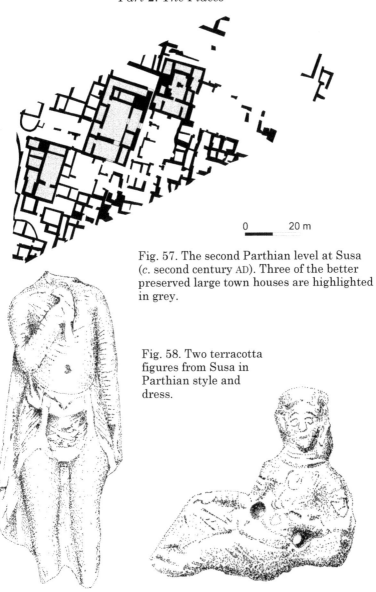

Fig. 57. The second Parthian level at Susa (*c.* second century AD). Three of the better preserved large town houses are highlighted in grey.

Fig. 58. Two terracotta figures from Susa in Parthian style and dress.

south. These houses are not the only evidence for Greeks living at Susa: Greek-style objects, such as pottery and terracotta figures, have been recovered from almost all parts of the city.

In the two Parthian levels were also found a number of impressive houses, certainly belonging to rich families. The houses in the first Parthian level (VI) are built side by side with little intervening space, though sometimes with smaller houses in between. This level is not so well preserved, and it is therefore not easy to form a clear picture of them or understand their internal arrangement. The houses in the second Parthian level are slightly better preserved, doubtless because the Sassanian level above it was much less densely occupied. In this level (V), dating to the second century AD, the houses had a similar plan to the Seleucid ones. In the bigger houses all rooms are arranged around an open courtyard. These courtyards are not square in shape, but elongated rectangles, and this seems to indicate that they were connected with an iwan: one part of the rectangle would be the roofed iwan, the other part the actual open court. The presence of smaller houses next to these large dwellings illustrates a certain social mixture in this part of town, not attested for the Seleucid level. At present, the overall plan of the Parthian city is not readily apparent. There is little evidence for any kind of street planning. Whereas the Hellenistic level seems to follow a grid plan with broader streets, only very small streets are detectable for the Parthian levels, although this feature might merely reflect the poor preservation of the overall plan.

Among the most interesting sources from these later periods are over thirty inscriptions in Greek on stone, from different parts of the city. They provide us with a direct view of Greek-Parthian urban life. They are a first-class source, in which the people of the time speak directly to us. Not many of the inscriptions were found well preserved, and the broken condition of most of them complicates attempts to grasp even the general message, but in their detail they still offer extremely useful evidence. Many of the inscriptions inform us about dedications of slaves to different gods:

> In year 171 (=142/1 BC), in the month [...] Straton, son of Simias, dedicated to the goddess Nanaya Kan[...], his young female slave, at 30 years (of age), for the preservation of the king and the queen, and let it not be permitted to Straton nor to any on his behalf in any way whatsoever to lay claim to the above mentioned slave nor to sell (?her). If he does any of these things, let it be invalid and let him pay besides to the temple of Nanaya 3000 drachmas of silver.[97]

Nanaya, mentioned in this text, is a Mesopotamia goddess, attested since Ur III period (around 2000 BC). She appears in four of the Greek inscriptions, and the mention of 'the goddess' on a fifth source may refer to her again. In Susa she does not appear with a temple of her own until the Seleucid period. Stones of the temple were found, indicating that it must have been an important building, and the Greek inscriptions suggest that she was the main deity worshipped here, at least by the Greeks. Greek gods are not mentioned so often. A few inscriptions are dedicated to Apollo, or at least mention him. Curiously, one dedication dates back to the sixth century BC: 'Aristolochus and Thrason dedicated these images to Apollo out of booty as a tenth-part; Isikles son of Kudimandros cast them'. This is inscribed on a solid-cast bronze knuckle-bone, presumably transported to the new city by trade or war; since Apollo appears in other dedications, it is possible that the knuckle-bone might have been offered as a votive to him a second time in its new home, in Seleucid or Parthian times. The mention of the various gods provides a clear picture of the general pattern in religious practice. Evidently the Greeks living in the city not only worshipped their own gods, but also followed the customs of the local people, at least in terms of the gods they worshipped.

Some Greek institutions are mentioned in the texts, showing that the Greeks imported many things from home: in one inscription a certain 'Nicolaos, son of Ma[cedon] winner in the games' refers to the stadium of the city.

A long letter by the Parthian king Artabanus II, preserved on a large stone slab, demonstrates that some of the Greek institutions still functioned under Parthian rule. The document is dated to year 268 (21 AD) of the Parthian era and is addressed to Antiochus and Phraates, who were the archons of the city. Archon is a Greek word, originally meaning simply 'ruler'. It is often the title of the highest or one of the highest officials in a town or city, best known from ancient Athens but also used as important title in the administration of other cities. Several times male or female slaves are mentioned in the texts. They are always dedicated for a period of 30 years to the temple of Nanaya, demonstrating that the slave economy continued in force, at least on the religious estates.

The Greek inscriptions date to the third to the first century BC. Only two are datable to the first century of the Christian era. This shows that Greek was still used till the first century AD, but also that, at about that time, Greek disappeared from official inscriptions.

In Susa were also found several sculptures, several of them purely Hellenistic, others in a more Parthian style.[98] A remarkable head from a figure of a woman is often assigned to queen Musa, although this is far from certain. It has been assumed that this high quality sculpture is an import from the Roman empire, and was just reworked in Susa.[99]

Fig. 59. Head found at Susa and often assigned to queen Musa.

Fig. 60. Terracotta figure from Susa, in a mixed Hellenistic-Parthian style.

Some information is available on the cemeteries of the city, although little detail has been published. East of the city proper there is a quarter named by the excavators 'ville des artisans'. Here were found remains of workshops, but also parts of an extensive cemetery. Three types of tombs were found. There are individual graves consisting of simple pits, where, besides the burials of adults, there were children and infants for whom storage jars were used as coffins. Only a few specially made pottery coffins were found, perhaps all for adults, and all belonging to the Parthian period. Funerary goods are rare. It is not clear from the published records whether these graves were placed in an area devoted exclusively to burials, or were placed under the floors of houses, as attested elsewhere. In both the main city and the 'ville des artisans' were found shaft tombs with a chamber at the bottom. In some of these were discovered the blue glazed pottery coffins, so typical of the Parthians. These tombs range in date from the third century BC to about the first century AD.

Underground chambers were the dominant feature in the typical tombs of the later Parthian period. They were dug immediately below the surface and had a staircase or a shaft. Shaft tombs generally had one or two vaulted chambers, while staircase tombs had three chambers, each of them with benches along the walls on which the coffins were placed. Although little is published, it seems that the deceased in these tombs were well equipped with funerary goods, such as vessels, glass bottles, terracotta figures, weapons and jewellery.[100]

Charax Spasinou

In archaeological terms, Babylonia is among the better researched areas in the world, and many of its most ancient sites have been identified and at least partly excavated. The main temples are known, and, as we have seen, in several places we can gain at least a fair idea of the living quarters of the population. Nevertheless, there are still many towns and villages not yet excavated at all. In particular, those belonging to the Parthian period have not yet attracted much attention from archaeologists. Charax Spasinou, the capital of Characene, is one important example. The city is mentioned several times in inscriptions and the ancient literature, and from these references it is certain that it was a major trading centre of the Gulf. In the ancient records it also appears with the name Mesene, which was one name for its region. The city has not yet been excavated, but in 1955-1956 archaeologists located the site, which covered a trapezoidal area measuring 2.8 x 1.5 x 1.3 x 2.9 km. It was protected by walls of fired bricks and earth, still in parts 4.6 m high.

From the ancient written sources it is possible to reconstruct at least some aspects of the life of the city. Pliny describes the town, lying between the Tigris and the Eulaios (a branch of the Tigris) on an artificial hill. The town was founded by Alexander the Great, and initially called Alexandria. The first settlers were Greeks and people from a royal city called Durine. As inhabitants he chose veteran soldiers who could not fight because of their old age or because of war injuries. Later the city was flooded, and the Seleucid king Antiochus IV rebuilt it and named it after himself: Antioch.[101] He also founded a mint in the city. This intervention should be seen in connection with specific political strategies on the part of the king. There are indications that he tried to support trade in this region, although the evidence is vague, such as the many coins of the king found at sites around the Gulf. Furthermore, Pliny reports that a governor of the Mesene named Numenius fought a sea-battle on the sea in the Gulf under a king Antiochus.[102] This was most likely Antiochus IV.[103]

The city was again destroyed, most likely by further flooding, although this is nowhere stated, and it had to be rebuilt once more, this time by Hyspaosines.[104] He renamed it Charax Spasinou ('Palisade of Hyspaosines'). It became the capital of the Characene, and an important port in international trade.

In its strategic position, and as centre of an autonomous vassal kingdom, the port attracted many foreigners of all races and religions, to visit and to live here. The city even appears in Christian sources. In the 'Acts of Thomas', reporting the deeds of Saint Thomas in India, the city Mesene is called the 'collection point of the traders from the east'.[105]

From Jewish sources we learn that there was also a Jewish community here.

However, the richest source for the city are inscriptions found in the Syrian trading city Palmyra. There, it was the custom for private individuals to erect statues in honour of themselves or others. The bases of the status were inscribed in two languages, Greek and Palmyran, and most often mentioned the event for which the statue was set up. As Palmyra was an important trading centre, often these inscriptions also mention other trading cities, including Charax Spasinou.

One of the earliest inscriptions belongs to a certain Zabdibol, son of Obayhan. It was once part of a statue base which was found at the agora, the central market place of Palmyra. The statue itself has not survived, perhaps because it was made of bronze and later melted down. The statue was erected, as stated in the inscription, by 'all Palmyrenean traders, who were in Charax Spasinou'. The inscription is dated to 50/1 or 70/1 AD and is one of the earliest attestations of trade contacts between the two cities.[106] Several similar inscriptions are known, showing that this contact was not an exception, but maintained on a regular basis over about two hundred years. Some of them mention caravans, providing evidence that the trade between Palmyra and Charax Spasinou was conducted overland, not by river. In another inscription, sadly not dated and heavily destroyed, the honoured individual is identified as the 'archon' in Mesene,[107] most likely in Spasinou Charax. The administrative title 'archon' might indicate that the city had a Greek-style administration even in the Parthian period. However, as the Palmyrenean inscription is written in Greek, the possibility should not be excluded that a Parthian title was translated here by the Greek term 'archon'.

A certain Soadu, son of Bolyada, must have been a highly influential person among these Syrian traders; an inscription found near Palmyra and dating around 140 to 147 AD, records that in Palmyra, Charax Spasinou, Vologesias and Genna altogether 17 statues were set up in his honour. Three of them were erected in Charax Spasinou, indicating that the city was richly adorned with statues of important people.[108]

When founded, the city seems to have been quite close to the Gulf, and its location was therefore perfect for a sea harbour. Over the centuries the shoreline silted up, until the sea was so far away that the overseas trade required a new river port; the site chosen for this was Forat, some 17 km south of Charax Spasinou. This relocation is recorded by classical authors, who mention other places as ports. Although it no longer benefited from its status as port at the Gulf, Charax Spasinou remained an important trading town, with little sign of decline. The city continued to flourish under the Sassanians and into the early Islamic period, as confirmed by the pottery collected from the surface of the site.

The high number of references to Charax Spasinou in Palmyrenean inscriptions underlines the importance of the city and its port in the trade connecting India with the Roman empire. The city was certainly once rich. Only future excavations can reveal the lost splendour of this place.

Ikaros

Ikaros is the Greek name for the small island now called Failaka, 20 km off the coast of modern Kuwait. Its Greek name was taken from that of the Aegean island where, according to Greek myth, Ikaros son of Daedalos fell to earth after flying too close to the sun. The Greeks thought that the islands were roughly the same shape. After the conquest of India, Alexander the Great returned west by the land route to Persia (327-325 BC). At the same time the generals Nearchus and Onesicritus were asked to find a sea route connecting the Indus river with the Euphrates and Tigris. In 324 BC Nearchos sailed along the coast of the Gulf and reached finally Susa. Alexander, now already back in Babylon, sent Nearchus on a second journey into the Gulf. According to the ancient historian Arrian, Nearchos 'discovered' Ikaros, though he may not have been in fact the first Greek to land on the island, for its long history connected it closely with the Mesopotamian and Persian worlds.

The island has been inhabited for several thousand years, with, notably, a settlement of the Dilmun culture, which flourished around 2000 BC in

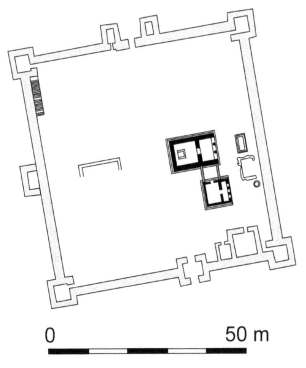

Fig. 61. The fortress or temple enclosure on Ikaros.

0   50 m

the Gulf region. Archaeological excavations on the island also revealed a Seleucid trading point of some importance. A fortress about 59 x 59m in area was built at the end of the fourth or the beginning of the third century BC, most likely in the reign of Seleucus I.[109] Inside the fortress walls were several separate buildings, including two small Greek temples in stone. In the second half of the third century BC some further buildings were added, and the walls and towers of the fortifications were strengthened. It has been assumed that these modifications were carried out under Antiochus III, who conquered several territories around the Gulf, such as Tylos (Bahrain) and the important trading city Gerrha on the Arabian mainland. Indeed around 187 BC the fortress seems to have been rebuilt after a fire, and this might be the moment from which it became an important naval base in the Gulf.

The temples excavated are of special interest because, though relatively small, they are so far the only known fully Greek-style temples in the entire region of the Gulf and Mesopotamia. The bigger and older one (A), founded around 260 BC, is about 7.5 x 12 m in area and was perhaps 6 m high. Built of limestone, it is a typical example of a Greek temple type called *templum in antis*. There is a cella (also called *naos*), where stood the statue of the god, of which the base is preserved. This is fronted by the *pronaos* with two columns, as is typical of this type of temple. The capitals of the columns are of classical Greek Ionic style. On the roof there were antefixes adorned with palmettes. The bases of the columns are interesting. They are not classical Greek but Persian, and similar to other examples found in the Achaemenid empire, such as in the palace built by Darius at Susa. These column bases are adorned with hanging foliage all around. The bases are made of a different type of stone to the rest of the columns, suggesting that they came originally from an Achaemenid building on the island, from which the materials were reused for this Greek temple.

Next to this temple stood a smaller one (temple B), of the same type, but in the Doric order, that is, with simple columns without base and plainer capitals. This temple is not well preserved. For both temples, it is not certain which deities were worshipped here. Apollo has been proposed for the bigger one, but this is nothing more than a guess.

Around the fortress are the remains of a settlement. So far only a few houses have been excavated, not enough to provide an overall impression of the site. However, these few remains indicate that it was not a densely populated town, but a rather loosely spread-out settlement area. One excavated house contained many high quality Greek-style terracotta figures along with the moulds for terracotta figures. It has therefore been assumed that this was the workshop where they were produced. This is not certain, but the high quality of the figures at this site certainly seems remarkable. Especially beautiful is the small statue of a sitting man, perhaps a king. It has been proposed that this figure shows Mithridates II. However, this is far from certain, and the crown depicted is not known for

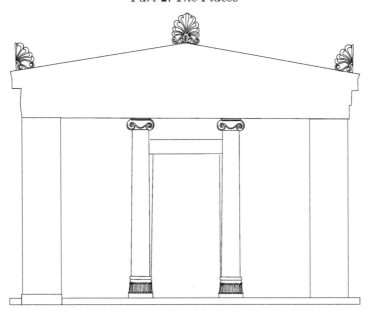

Fig. 62. Reconstruction of the main temple found on Ikaros, Failaka.

Fig. 63. Statuette of a
Parthian king, perhaps
Mithridates II.

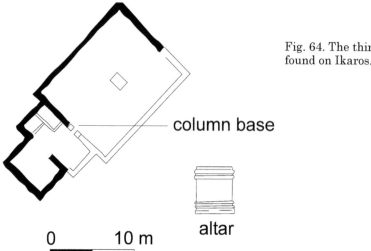

Fig. 64. The third temple found on Ikaros.

column base

altar

0   10 m

that king. Perhaps a local artist just made an image of a Parthian king without having a particular king in mind.[110]

About 100 m south of the fortress were found the remains of a third temple. By comparison with the two described, it is more simple, no columns were found and the plan is rather irregular. Several altars were discovered, there was also pottery and there were some terracotta figures, several in Greek style. This sanctuary bears all the hallmarks of a local cult, perhaps even specifically for indigenous inhabitants, while the two temples in the fort are classical Greek and certainly built by and for Greeks living here, and may even have been erected by higher authorities.

A few Greek inscriptions were found on Ikaros. The longest is the copy of a letter of a certain Anarchus to the people of Ikaros. It dates to year 71 of the Seleucid era (241 BC).

It is hard to get a clear picture from life on Ikaros under Seleucid rule from this rather sparse evidence. It is not known how long the settlement or colony survived. Most of the coins found belong to the Seleucid era, but there are also a few coins of kings of Characene. Since more southerly islands belonged to Characene, that kingdom seems most likely to have included Ikaros too. Apparently, the settlement flourished especially under Seleucid rule, but later lost its significance, even though people certainly still lived here. Perhaps it was only a naval station under the Greeks, while later state authorities left the site and relocated their naval bases elsewhere. With such a move, many people might have left the island to find new homes. The pottery uncovered on the island is very close in style to that found in southern Mesopotamia. This is in contrast to the other important island in the Gulf, Bahrain, where different pottery traditions appear.[111]

The evidence from Ikaros is of an importance that belies its small scale.

It is one of the few places within the Seleucid empire where Greek-style temples have been found. In contrast, the Seleucid temples at Uruk were still built in a fully Mesopotamian style, doubtless because most of the population here was not Greek and followed old traditions. On Ikaros a higher percentage of the population was most probably of Greek origin, in particular a significant proportion of the ruling class. Here, with its Greek temples, a mixture of cultures is not yet really visible.

Tylos (Bahrain)

Tylos is the Greek name for Bahrain, the largest island in the Persian Gulf. In cuneiform texts from about 2300 BC onwards, the island and its maritime region is called Dilmun. It was certainly an important post on the trade routes between India and Mesopotamia. The name Tylos in the Greek sources might be the Greek adaptation of the Sumerian word Dilmun (Tilmun).

It is uncertain whether it was part of the Seleucid empire. Antiochus III undertook a major military campaign in the Gulf, during which his forces looted the rich trading city Gerrha, located on the Arabian peninsula. With this campaign one wonders whether he also occupied Bahrain. At least for the Parthian period it seems certain, from two inscriptions, that the island belonged to Characene. There is an inscription in Greek found on the island naming king Hyspaosines of Characene and his wife, recording the building of a temple for the Dioscuri. The monument was set up by the strategos of 'Tylos and the islands' Cephisodorus. Before becoming king, Hyspaosines was governor of the 'satrapy of the Erythraean Sea';[112] this satrapy was installed by Antiochus III, further evidence, beside his military campaign in this region, that his reign saw the incorporation of Bahrain into the Seleucid empire. An inscription from Palmyra dating to 131 AD shows that the king of Characene, Meredates, appointed Yarhai as satrap of the people of Thilouna, another name for the 'people of Tylos' (Bahrain).[113] Finally, the Persian historian Tibari (839-923) mentions that there was a certain king Sanatruq on Tylos, who was eliminated by the Sassanian king Ardashir I. However, from the indications mentioned above, Sanatruq was perhaps not an independent ruler, but rather a Parthian governor.[114]

From this evidence, it seems certain that the island was part of Characene, and we will see that the material culture on the island shows strong Parthian influence, when it is not indeed directly identifiable as Parthian.

Archaeology again provides the main sources for our knowledge of life on the island. The major ancient town is situated towards its northern tip. Its modern name is Qal'at al-Bahrain. Its ancient name was Tylos, as Pliny reported.[115] The Greek Theophrastus (c. 371-287 BC) provided a longer description of the island.[116] As one of the first writers interested in plants, he reports that cotton grew on the island. Otherwise cotton was little known in the Greek world, and Theophrastos calls it the 'wool-bearing' tree. Pliny mentions that the island was famous for pearls.[117]

The town on Bahrain was already of some importance by around 2300 BC, and may have been the capital of the Dilmun civilisation. The site of the town covers an area of about 300 x 600 m. People lived there till the Middle Ages, when the Portuguese built a large fortress over it. About one quarter of the city has so far been excavated; unfortunately, the Greek and Parthian levels are especially badly preserved. Little of the architecture has survived, and it has been argued that the houses were built of a light material, which would explain why they are now entirely gone.[118] It has been calculated that in the Seleucid and Parthian periods about 8,000 people lived on Bahrain, of which a high percentage perhaps resided in the city, because there are not many other settlement sites known from this period on the island.[119] There is pottery dating to the Seleucid and Parthian periods, demonstrating that the town was still populated then. This is confirmed by the numerous coins of kings from Characene and the Parthian empire known from the island. They do not prove direct rule by those kings, but are at least evidence of close contacts. Beside the trade in pearls, the island might have served as watering point and station on the sea route to India.[120]

An interesting report on life in the Persian Gulf was written by Isidore of Charax, and preserved in a later reference. He describes the life of pearl fishers with unusual detail, in a passage worth citing at length:

> Isidore of Charax in his description of Parthia says there is a certain island in the Persian Gulf where many pearls are found; and that round about the island there are rafts made of reeds, from which men dive into the sea to a depth of 20 fathoms [*c.* 30 m] and bring up double-shelled oysters. They say that when there are frequent thunderstorms and heavy rains, the oyster produces the most young, and they get the most, the best and the largest pearls; and in the winter the shells are accustomed to sink into holes in the bottom, but in the summer they swim about all night with their shells open, but they close in the daytime. And when they cling to stones and rocks in the waves they take root and then, remaining fixed, produce the pearls. These are engendered and nourished by something that adheres to their flesh. It grows in the mouth of the oyster and has claws and brings in food. It is like a small crab and is called 'Guardian of the oyster'. Its flesh penetrates through the centre of the shell like a root; the pearl being engendered close to it, grows through the solid portion of the shell and keeps growing as long as it continues to adhere to the shell. But when the flesh gets under the excrescence and cuts its way onward, it gently separates the pearl from the shell and then, when the pearl is surrounded by flesh, it is no longer nourished in such manner as to grow further, but the flesh makes it smoother, more transparent and more pure. And when the oyster lives at the bottom, it produces the clearest and largest pearls; but those that float on the surface, because they are affected by the rays of the sun, produce smaller pearls, of poorer colour. The pearl divers run into danger when they thrust

their hands straight into the open oyster, for it closes up and their fingers are often cut off, and sometimes they perish on the spot; but those who take them by thrusting their hands under from one side, easily pull the shells off from the rocks.[121]

The most prominent archaeological and still visible features all over the island are several thousand small mounds which were erected over tombs. Many of them were excavated and a quite high number belong to the Greek and Parthian periods, although little has yet been published,[122] and it is even not sure whether the Parthian tombs were covered by mounds in the manner of the earlier period. On Bahrain, where parts of the island are desert, the preservation conditions for organic materials are sometimes good. Here objects survived that are not known from other parts of south Mesopotamia and the Persian Gulf. On the island there were found, for example, several wooden coffins. These coffins are plain wooden boxes with a triangular-section lid. This type of coffin is well known from Ptolemaic and Roman Egypt. It seems to represent a type that originally came from Greece, although only a few examples survived there, whereas several are known from Egypt with its much better preservation conditions for wood. Evidently, the burial customs of the region were influenced by Greek traditions. The burials were often placed into rough stone cists. They appear in clusters, with the impression that there was a first, main burial and then other burials which followed. At the beginning of the Greek period the bodies were oriented east to west, later without any visible order. In general these tombs provide a rich array of objects of daily life placed next to the dead. The dead were most likely buried with their daily clothing and accessories, such as personal adornments. In the tombs of men were found weapons, in the burials of women cosmetic objects. These things doubtless recreated for eternity the social identity of these people. Rich people had distinctly more expensive objects in their graves than the poor. For most burials pottery vessels were provided. Some remains of food were found in or next to them. This presumably assured an kind of eternal food supply, but it is also possible that it comes from a

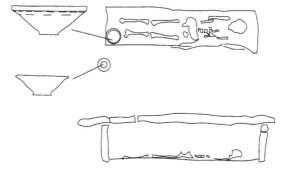

Fig. 65. Tomb no. 4 at the cemetery of Janussan (Bahrain). The undisturbed tomb contained the body of a man about 30 years old.

funerary meal. Another option is that food and drink were placed there as an offering to underworld deities. The vessels found are often typical of Parthian production, but there are also many local types. Burials of children are most often rather plain, and contain nothing more than a few pots. A large number of burials were placed in rectangular stone boxes covered with stones. In some burials a coin was found near the mouth of the deceased. This is clearly the ancient Greek tradition of providing an obol to pay the underworld ferryman Charon.[123]

One cemetery on Bahrain was found at a place today called Shakhura, about 3 km south-west of Qal'at al-Bahrain. Perhaps some wealthy inhabitants of the town were buried here. One mound (mound 1) with 90 graves was excavated from October 1996 to March 1997. An example of a well preserved grave is burial 2. It belonged to an adult woman and was found undisturbed. She was placed on her back. Around her neck was found a necklace consisting of eight golden beads decorated with golden balls, almost providing the impression of grapes or other small clusters of fruit. Other beads on the necklace were made of rock crystal, amethyst and carnelian, but are simpler, oval or round in shape. The two end pieces are golden tubes. She was wearing simple gold earrings and on her left hand was found a golden ring showing a cameo with a face. Near her right hand carnelian and agate beads were found. There was a bone spindle and a cosmetic case in shape of a long tube made of bone.[124]

Another necklace comes from grave 47, the burial of a girl, and is made of gold. It consists of a series of beads decorated with granulation, which is an ancient gold-working technology. Tiny golden balls are soldered onto a golden surface to form geometric patterns, in this instance triangles. In the same tomb was found a stylised bone figure of a woman. Similar figures are known from many parts of the Parthian world. Glass vessels were also found in the tomb.[125]

Glass vessels are among the most beautiful objects found in tombs on Bahrain. Most of them seem to be imports from the eastern part of the Roman empire, again showing strong trading links with the Mediterranean world.[126] Other vessels are Parthian, and show the typical green-blue glazing.[127] Perhaps of local production are some stone vessels made of calcite.[128]

From another tomb comes a pair of golden earrings. At the top of each is a figure of Eros, the Greek god of love, riding on a goat. From the underside of the goat hangs a golden disk with a pearl in the middle, from which there hangs in turn a model of an amphora. The body consists of a green stone, while the upper part, the neck of the vessel, is made of gold with two handles and there is separate golden vase-foot.[129] It is not known where this pair of earrings was made, perhaps in a Parthian city or even in Bactria. These tombs clearly demonstrate the wealth of at least some people living on the island. The glass vessels and jewellery are all of highest quality. Both the Indian trade and the pearl trade were very important aspects of economic life for Characene and the Parthian empire in general. Pliny complained that fifty million sesterces went every year to India.[130] While that trade with the Roman empire was mainly conducted via Egypt, the trade routes via the Persian Gulf were important too.

Another common ancient Greek tradition was to place a stela with an inscription or a picture of the deceased over the tomb. Such a custom is so far not known of the Dilmun people before the arrival of Alexander the Great. However, there are several stone objects known from the island which most likely served as tombstones, providing direct evidence for further strong cultural influence from another part of the ancient world.

There are two types of tomb stela. There are stelae which are very roughly human-shaped, with a highly stylised body, reduced to a simple rectangle topped by a roundel for the head, with no further details. Some of these bear a Greek inscription. Other stelae are much more elaborate, showing the deceased in bold relief. The stelae with the reliefs are of special interest. As indicated, the island was most likely part of Characene. Few objects are known from mainland Characene which could be classified as art, and the Bahrain stelae belong to the few sources providing at least a glimpse of art production in the vassal kingdom of Characene. In general two styles can be distinguished. There are stelae which seem very much in a Hellenistic tradition. One example is the stela of a young man. In his right hand he carries grapes, in his left he holds a bird. He has short curly hair and no moustache or beard. He wears a chiton, a typical Greek dress. Other stelae are more in a style known from other places as Parthian. One stela shows a man with a full beard, a moustache and full curly hair. The men on these stelae most often raise a hand in worship, a gesture well known from statues found at Hatra in Mesopotamia. The left hand quite often holds a piece of cloth, folded and placed over the shoulder. Similar depictions are known from Elymais. Furthermore the stelae show some connections to contemporary Phoenician stelae. A Phoenician connection to the island is also mentioned by Strabo (16.3.4), who mentions that there were on Bahrain temples like those of the Phoenicians. The evidence attests to links with the eastern Mediterranean.[131] The worksmanship of these stelae varies. Some are described as of fair quality, others are rather clumsy. Nevertheless, if we take these depictions of the people of Bahrain seriously, they offer a good idea of how the people of Bahrain saw themselves. The upper classes there followed Greek and Parthian fashions. It is not known where these stelae were produced. Bahrain itself seems to be the most likely place, but for the higher quality examples Characene can not be excluded.

We do not know much about the end of the Parthian era on Bahrain. At one point a substantial fortress was built in Qal'at al-Bahrain. Its date is unknown. It has been assumed that the fortress is Parthian, but it is also possible that it was Sassanian, marking a new period in the history of the island.

Bahrain also yielded invaluable information on the living conditions of

Fig. 66. Limestone stela found on Bahrain, *c*. 36 cm high. The style of this piece is provincial but still very much under Greek influence.

Fig. 67. Limestone stela found on Bahrain, 46 cm high. The man shown is depicted in typical Parthian style.

Fig. 68. Stela found on Bahrain. The man depicted is similar to the one in Fig. 67 but much simpler in style and rather out of proportion, obviously made by a local workshop. He raises his right hand in worship and holds part of his garment with his left hand. Several such provincial stelae were found on Bahrain.

people. Many burials and skeletons were excavated in the region under discussion, but so far only for Bahrain is there a published study examining all the skeletal material, the most direct evidence for the population existing on this island. As in all pre-industrial societies, child mortality was high. For every 100 infants, defined as children up to the age of one year, about 38 died, only 62 survived. On reaching their second year, children had a higher chance of surviving longer. There is again a high mortality rate for women aged between 20 and 30. As men did not have the same fate in this age, this evidently relates to maternal mortality at childbirth. At the age of between 30 and 40 women still died at a higher rate than men, although not as much as in their younger years. Only a few people reached what we might consider old age. Only 2.5% of the women and 4.5% of men lived longer than 50 years.[132]

*

History is still too often divided into first-level and second-level nations and empires. A visit to any bookshop will yield plenty of publications on the Roman empire, but little on other contemporary kingdoms. The same is true for many so-called 'world art history' books – the Parthians and many lesser known people are often not mentioned at all. In this book, I have presented one of the lesser known empires of the ancient world and the lives of its people. Parthian sculpture and painting influenced European art for the next thousand years. Put the 'Offering of Konon', a painting found at Dura Europos,[133] directly next to the mosaic at Ravenna depicting the emperor Justinian, and you will see striking similarities in style and composition. Parthian architecture and stucco decoration also formed the basis for Islamic architecture. I hope that this study helps to correct our often narrow view of the ancient world.

Lists of Kings

Seleucid Kings (to 125 BC)

Seleucus I Nicator	305-281 BC
Antiochus I Soter	281-261 BC
Antiochus II Theoas	261-246 BC
Seleucus II Callinicus	246-225 BC
Seleucus III Soter	225-223 BC
Antiochus III, the great	223-187 BC
Seleucus IV Philopator	187-175 BC
Antiochus IV Epiphanes	175-164 BC
Antiochus V Eupator	164-162 BC
Demetrius I Soter	162-150 BC
Alexander Balas	150-145 BC
Demetrius II Nicator	145-138 BC
Antiochus VI Dionysus	145-142 BC
Antiochus VII Sidetes	138-129 BC
Demetrius II Nicator	129-125 BC

Parthian Kings

Arsaces I	*c.* 247/38-217 BC
Arsaces II	*c.* 217-191 BC
Phriapatius	*c.* 191-176 BC
Phraates I	176-171 BC
Mithridates I	171-139/8 BC
Phraates II	139/8-128 BC
Artabanus I	128-124/3 BC
Mithridates II	124/3-88/7 BC
Gotarzes I	91/0-81/0 BC
Orodes I	81/0-76/5 BC
Sinatruces	*c.* 78/7-71/0 BC
Phraates III	71/0-58/7 BC
Mithridates III	58/7 BC
Orodes II	58/7-38 BC
Phraates IV	38-3/2 BC
Phraates V	2 BC - 2 AD
Orodes III	4-6 AD
Vonones I	8/9 AD
Artabanus II	10/1-38 AD
Vardanes	38-45 AD
Gotarzes II	43/4-51 AD

Vonones II	51 AD
Vologases I	51-76/80 AD
Pacorus	77/8-108/9 AD
Vologases II	77/8 AD
Artabanus III	79-81 AD
Osroes	108/9-127/8 AD
Vologases III	111/2-147/8 AD
Vologases IV	147/8-191/2 AD
Vologases V	191/2-207/8 AD
Vologases VI	207/8-221/2 or 227/8 AD
Artabanus IV	213-224 AD

Kings of Characene

Hyspaosines	*c.* 127-124 BC
Apodacus	*c.* 110/9-104/3 BC
Tiraius I	95/4-90/89 BC
Tiraius II	79/8-49/8 BC
Artabazus I	49/8-48/7 BC
Attambelus I	47/6-25/4 BC
Theonesius I	25/4-19/8 BC
Attambelus II	*c.* 17/6 BC - AD 8/9
Abinergaus I	10/1; 22/3 AD
Orabazes I	*c.* 19 AD
Attambelus III	*c.* 37/8-44/5 AD
Theonesius II	*c.* 46/7 AD
Theonesius III	*c.* 52/3 AD
Attambelus IV	54/5-64/5 AD
Attambelus V	64/5-73/4 AD
Orabazes II	*c.* 73-80 AD
Pacorus (II)	80-101/2 AD
Attambelus VI	*c.* 101/2-105/6 AD
Theonesius IV	*c.* 110/1-112/3 AD
Attambelus VII	113/4-117 AD
Meredates	*c.* 131-150/1 AD
Orabazes III	*c.* 150/1-165 AD
Abinergaus II (?)	*c.* 165-180 AD
Attambelus VIII	*c.* 180-195 AD
Maga (?)	*c.* 195-210 AD
Abinergaus III	*c.* 210-222 AD

Kings of Elymais
Note: the number and succession of these kings is very uncertain.

Kamnaskires I Soter	*c.* 147 BC
Kamnaskires II Nikephoros	*c.* 145-139 BC
Okkonapses	*c.* 139 BC
Tigraios	138/7-133/2 BC
Kamnaskires III	82/1-75 BC

Kamnaskires IV	62/1 or 59/8 and 56/5 BC
Kamnaskires V	36/5 BC
Orodes I	first half first century AD
Phraates	end first/or beginning of second century AD
Orodes II	first half second century AD
Kamnaskires-Orodes III	second half first century AD
Osroes/ Chosroes (?)	second century AD
Orodes IV	second century AD
(A)Bar-Basi	second century AD?

Glossary

agora (Greek): meeting place and market place in Greek cities.

antefix: vertical element which terminates the covering tiles of a tiled roof.

Antum: Mesopotamian goddess, wife of Anu.

Anu (also **An**): city god of Uruk; a sky deity and father of all gods that came after him.

archon: highest official in the administration of a Greek city.

Astronomical Diaries: records from Babylon describing astronomical observations and also political events which were thought to have been predicted by the celestial omens.

Bel (also **Baal**): means 'lord' or 'master' and refers in several Semitic cities to their main deity

blind arcade: a series of arches with actual no openings and that is applied to the surface of a wall as a purely decorative element.

caravan: a group of people travelling together, most often on a trade mission.

chiton: Greek dress worn by men and women.

eparchos: (Greek) governor of a province.

herm: a sculpture, most often showing a man with a head, and perhaps a torso, above a plain, usually squared lower section, on which male genitals may also be carved at the appropriate height. They were originally cult images for the Greek god Hermes.

iwan: a vaulted hall or space, walled on three sides, with one side entirely open.

obverse: the front of a coin, in antiquity often bearing a portrait of a ruler.

palmette: artistic motif which resembles the fan-shaped leaves of a palm tree.

pinax (plural **pinakes**): votive tablet made of wood, terracotta or other materials.

reverse: the back side of a coin.

satrap: the governor of a province in the Achaemenid Empire; the term was still used in the Seleucid and Parthian administrations.

stoa (Greek): covered walkway, often with columns on one side.

Stoicism: a school of Hellenistic philosophy founded in Athens by Zeno of Citium in the early third century BC.

tetradrachm: Greek coin, equivalent to four drachmae, widely used throughout the ancient Greek world.

vassal state: a state subordinate to another state.

Notes

Introduction

1. Herzfeld 1934, 50-2.
2. Mathiesen 1992, 13.
3. Colledge 1967, 143.
4. Roux & Renger 2005, 240.
5. Wirth 1934, 10.
6. Schlumberger, 1969, 217-23.
7. Bickerman 1943.

Part 1. The Historical Setting

1. Diodorus 18.7.3; Holt 1993, 88-9.
2. Potts 1990, 17-19.
3. Ehling 2008, 124-9.
4. Ehling 2008, 182-3.
5. Ehling 2008, 183-5.
6. Ehling 2008, 201-5.
7. One example are the four (or more) books on Parthian history by Apollodorus of Artemita, only preserved in later quotations.
8. Wolski 1993, 13.
9. Justin 41.4.
10. Strabo 11.9.3.
11. Photius (Bibl. codex 58.1-3); for the events in general see Lerner 1999, 13-19.
12. Wolski 1993, 74.
13. Wolski 1993, 79-83; Curtis 2007, 11.
14. Curtis 2007, 9.
15. Ehling 2008, 182-3.
16. Ehling 2008, 184-5.
17. Justin 42.1; Wolski 1993, 87.
18. Wolski 1988, 159-66; Wolski 1993, 97-8; Curtis 2007, 14-15.
19. van der Spek 1998, 212, 215-24.
20. The Sassanian empire lasted from 224 to 642, i.e. 418 years. The Parthian empire lasted from 247 BC to 224 AD, i.e. 471 years. However, it must be admitted that for its first 100 years the Parthian empire was a small, rather minor kingdom.
21. Wang Tao 2007, 87-104; Schuol 2000, 450.
22. Kose 1998, 415.
23. Wolski 1993, 127-34.
24. Josephus Flavius, *Antiquities of the Jews* 18.2.4; Wolski 1993, 147-8.
25. Strugnell 2008.
26. Finkbeiner 1993, 285.
27. Mathiesen 1992, 15.
28. Curtis 2007.
29. Tacitus, *Annals* 6.31.

30. Tacitus, *Annals* 6.37, 43, 44.
31. Bivar 2007, 32.
32. Curtis 2007, 16.
33. For peasant revolts in general see de Ste. Croix 1981, 474-88.
34. Justin 41.2.
35. Josephus Flavius, *Antiquities of the Jews*, 18.310-79; Neusner 1969, 54-7; Rajak 1998, 314-17.
36. Unless otherwise stated this outline follows Schuol 2000.
37. Gatier et al. 2002, 223-26.
38. Strabo 16.1.18.
39. Dabrowa 1998, 417; the following summary of its history follows basically Potts 1999, 375-409.
40. Dabrowa 1998, 417.
41. Potts 1999, 253-6.
42. Potts 1999, 373.
43. Strabo 11.13.6; Potts 1999, 380.
44. Polybius 5.48; Potts 1999, 355.
45. Potts 1999, 383 (with further references); Mittag 2006, 307-10.
46. Le Rider 1965, 349.
47. Le Rider 1965, 236, 346-7 (there called Hyknopses); Ehling 2008, 130 (there called Hyknapses). Le Rider dates him much earlier, around 162-160 BC. Ehling and others follow him.
48. Le Rider 1965, 378-81.
49. Le Rider 1965, 81-3.
50. Potts 1999, 392, 399.
51. Against that view, the evidence from cuneiform texts mentioning Parthian kings and their wives must be mentioned. The king's mother does not appear here (McEwan 1986, 93).
52. McEwan 1986.
53. Strabo 16.1.18.
54. Alram 1998, 371.
55. Schuol 2000, 62-3.
56. Mathiesen 1992, 133-5.
57. Some publications also distinguish Orodes IV and Orodes V.
58. Dabrowa 1998, 421.
59. Potts 1999, 412.

Part 2. The Places

1. Strabo 11.13.1.
2. Boiy 2004, 135.
3. Pliny, *Nat. Hist.* 6.122.
4. Tacitus, *Annals* 6.42.
5. Boiy 2004, 135 (Strabo 16.1.5; Pausanias 1.16.3; Pliny, *Nat. Hist.* 6.122).
6. Tacitus, *Annals* 11.8.
7. Rajak 1998, 314-17; Josephus, *Antiquities of the Jews* 18.310-78.
8. Cassius Dio 68.30.
9. Cassius Dio 71.2.
10. Cassius Dio 76.9.
11. Colledge 1967, 120; Schlumberger 1969, 120; Colledge 1977, 63-4.
12. Wirth 1934, 25; Baldassarre et al. 2002, 67-74.

13. Baldassarre et al. 2002, 80-9.

14. van Ingen 1939, 354, no. 1652, pl. 88, 644; Stucky 1977, no. 163.

15. Debevoise 1943, nos 358, 378, 369 (the pottery found is published in one volume and is selective).

16. Debevoise 1943, no. 31.

17. Debevoise 1943, no. 153.

18. For Parthian furniture in general see Curtis 1996.

19. Mathiesen 1992, fig. 17 on pp. 133, 135.

20. Curtis 1996, 235-6.

21. Mathiesen 1992, fig. 27 on p. 153.

22. Kawami 1987, 186, no. 26, pl. 31.

23. Curtis 1998.

24. Neusner 1969, 102.

25. Plutarch, *Life of Crassus* 24.

26. Boiy 2004, 105-6.

27. Strabo 15.3.9-10.

28. Wetzel et al. 1957, 3; compare the comments on further reference in Boiy 2004, 12 (the identification of the funeral pyre is not that certain).

29. Boiy 2004, 110.

30. Strabo 16.1.5.

31. Wetzel et al. 1957, 2-3.

32. *BCHP* (= *Babylonian Chronicles of the Hellenistic Period*) 6 (compare for a recent discussion: http://www.livius.org/cg-cm/chronicles/bchp-ruin_esagila/ruin_esagila_01.html retrieved 11/12/2009).

33. Price 1991, 453-7.

34. Boardman 1994, 75-6, fig. 4.1 (assigns the coin to the mint at Babylon), this is not certain, Price 1991, 452.

35. Boiy 2004, 118-19.

36. Boiy 2004, 114.

37. Boiy 2004, 135.

38. Boiy 2004, 136.

39. Boiy 2004, 141-2.

40. After Wetzel et al. 1957, 29; compare Boiy 2004, 144.

41. Boiy 2004, 216.

42. Boiy 2004, 167.

43. Boiy 2004, 171.

44. Justin 42.1; Diodorus Siculus 34.21.

45. Boiy 2004, 180-1.

46. Schuol 2000, 50-1.

47. Livy 38.17.

48. Boiy 2004, 51.

49. Boiy 2004, 188.

50. Boiy 2004, 196-292.

51. Boiy 2004, 204-6.

52. Wetzel et al. 1957, 26.

53. Wetzel et al. 1957, 27.

54. Wetzel et al. 1957, 26, pl. 24c.

55. Wetzel et al. 1957, 24-5.

56. Wetzel et al. 1957, 25, 46, pl. 29.

57. Wetzel et al. 1957, 25.

58. Wetzel et al. 1957, 19-22.

59. Wetzel et al. 1957, 3-22; Boiy 2004, 188.
60. Boiy 2004, 93-4.
61. Wetzel et al. 1957, 22.
62. Diodorus Siculus 34.21.
63. Hauser 1999, 212.
64. Hauser 1999, 219.
65. Wetzel et al. 1957, 3-4.
66. Reuther 1926, 36-9.
67. Reuther 1926, 80-92.
68. For a summary of the evidence see Hauser 1999.
69. Wetzel et al. 1957, 31-3.
70. Wetzel et al. 1957, 34-45.
71. Reuther 1926, 251-2.
72. Reuther 1926, 249-65.
73. Adams 1981, 178.
74. Kose 1998, 186-7.
75. Kose 1998, 188.
76. Kose 1998, 189.
77. Finkbeiner 1991, 211-14.
78. Kose 1998, 23.
79. Kose 1998, 23.
80. Kose 1998, 51, 253-5.
81. Kose 1998, 55.
82. Mathiesen 1992, 188; Kose 1998, 334, pl. 166-7 (bronze feet KF 1077, 1097; limestone statue KF 1103).
83. Kose 2000.
84. Strabo 16.1.1.
85. Kose 1998, 243-51.
86. Schuol 2000, 66-9.
87. Mathiesen 1992, 78-80.
88. Kose 1998, 204.
89. Kose 1998, 210, 213, fig. 130.
90. Loftus 1857, 211.
91. Strabo 15.3.9-11.
92. Diodorus Siculus 19.13.6.
93. Schuol 2000, 62-3.
94. Potts 1999, 401-2.
95. Boucharlat 1993, 41-3.
96. Potts 1999, 370.
97. Translation after Potts 1999, 367.
98. Amiet 2001.
99. Kawami 1987, 53-6; Mathiesen 1992, 169 n. 2.
100. Boucharlat 1993, 43-4.
101. Pliny, *Nat. Hist.* 6.139; Schuol 2000, 280; Mittag 2006, 301-2.
102. Pliny, *Nat. Hist.* 6.152.
103. Mittag 2006, 305.
104. Pliny, *Nat. Hist.* 6.139.
105. Schuol 2000, 165-6.
106. Schuol 2000, 51-2.
107. Schuol 2000, 63-4.
108. Schuol 2000, 66-9.

109. Callot 1991, 121.

110. Cf. Mathiesen 1992, 21.

111. Finkbeiner 1993, 281-3.

112. Gatier et al. 2002, 223.

113. Schuol 2000, 56-7.

114. Crawford & Rice 2000, 135.

115. Pliny, *Nat. Hist.* 6.32.

116. Potts 1990, 129-30.

117. Pliny, *Nat. Hist.* 6.32.

118. Andersen 2007, 237.

119. Littleton 1998, 21.

120. Schuol 2000, 403.

121. Translation from Parthia.com (retrieved 23 March 2007): http://www.parthia.com/parthian_stations.htm; quoted from Athenaeus 3.46; compare Yonge 1854, 155-6.

122. Herling & Salles 1993, 162.

123. Summary on the burial customs: A. Herling in Crawford & Rice 2000, 136-41; Andersen 2007, 239-40.

124. Crawford & Rice 2000, 145, 164, no. 265, 166, no. 270, 182, no. 320; 183, no. 322, 185, no. 325.

125. Crawford & Rice 2000, 166, no. 256, 184, no. 323.

126. Crawford & Rice 2000, 167-77; Andersen 2007, 17-96.

127. Crawford & Rice 2000, 152-61.

128. Crawford & Rice 2000, 162-3.

129. Crawford & Rice 2000, 179, no. 307.

130. Pliny, *Nat. Hist.* 6.101.

131. Andersen 2007, 240.

132. Littleton 1998, 115-21.

133. Schlumberger 1969, fig. on p. 109.

Bibliography

Adams, R.M.C. & Nissen, H.J. (1972), *The Uruk Countryside*, London.

Adams, R.M.C. (1981), *Heartland of Cities*, Chicago & London.

Alram, M. (1998), 'Stand und Aufgaben der arsakidischen Numasmatik', in J. Wiesehöfer (ed.), *Das Partherreich und seine Zeugnisse*, Stuttgart: 365-87.

Amiet, P. (2001), 'La sculpture Susienne à l'époque de l'empire Parthe', *Iranica Antiqua* 36: 239-91.

Andersen, S.F. et al. (2004), 'Two wooden coffins from the Shakhoura Necropolis, Bahrain', *Arabian Archaeology and Epigraphy* 15: 219-28.

Andersen, S.F. (2007), *The Tylos Period Burials in Bahrain,* vol. 1: *The Glass and Pottery Vessels*, Bahrain.

Baldassarre, I., Pontrandolfo, A., Rouveret, A. &. Salvadori, M. (2002), *Pittura romana. Dall' ellenismo al tardo-antico*, Milan.

Bickerman, E.J. (1943), 'Notes on Seleucid and Parthian chronology', *Berytus Archeological Studies* VIII/II: 73-83.

Bivar, A.D.H. (2007), 'Gondophares and the Indo-Parthians', in V.S. Curtis & S. Stewart, *The Age of the Parthians: The Idea of Iran II*, London: 26-36.

Boardman, J. (1994), *The Diffusion of Classcial Art in Antiquity*, London.

Boiy, T. (2004), *Late Achaemenid and Hellenistic Babylon*, Orientalia Lovaniensia Analecta 136, Leuven.

Boucharlat, R. (1993), 'Pottery in Susa during the Seleucid, Parthian and early Sassanian periods', in U. Finkbeiner (ed.), *Materialien zur Archäologie der Seleukiden- und Partherzeit im südlichen Babylonien und im Golfgebiet*, Tübingen: 41-57.

Callot, O. (1991), 'La fortresse hellénistique de Failaka', in K. Schippmann, A. Herling & J.-F. Salles (eds), *Golf-Archäologie: Mesopotamien, Iran, Kuwait, Bahrain, Vereinigte Arabische Emirate und Oman*, Buch am Erlbach: 121-32.

Colledge, M.A.R. (1967), *The Parthians*, London.

Colledge, M.A.R. (1977), *Parthian Art*, London.

Crawford, H. & Rice, M (eds) (2000), *Traces of Paradise: The Archaeology of Bahrain, 2500 BC-300 AD*, London.

Curtis V.S. (1996), 'Parthian and Sasanian furniture', in G. Herrmann (ed.), *The Furniture of Western Asia, Ancient and Traditional*, Mainz.

Curtis V.S. (1998), 'The Parthian costume and headdress', in Josef Wiesehöfer (ed.), *Das Partherreich und seine Zeugnisse*, Stuttgart: 61-73.

Curtis, V.S. (2001), 'Parthian belts and belt plaques', *Iranica Antiqua* 36: 299-327.

Curtis V.S. (2007), 'The Iranian revival in the Parthian reriod', in V.S. Curtis & S. Stewart, *The Age of the Parthians: The Idea of Iran II*, London: 7-25.

Dbrowa, E. (1998), 'Zeugnisse zur Geschichte der parthischen Elymais und Susiane', in J. Wiesehöfer (ed.), *Das Partherreich und seine Zeugnisse*, Stuttgart: 417-24.

Debevoise, N.C. (1934), *Parthian Pottery from Seleucia on the Tigris*, Ann Arbor.

Ehling, K. (2008), *Untersuchungen zur Geschichte der späten Seleukiden (164-63 v. Chr.)*, Stuttgart.

Finkbeiner, U. (1991), *Uruk, Kampagne 35-37, 1982-1984, Die archäologischen Oberfläschenfunde (Survey)*, Mainz am Rhein.

Finkbeiner, U. (1993), 'Vergleichende Stratigraphie und Chronologie', in U. Finkbeiner (ed.), *Materialien zur Archäologie der Seleukiden- und Partherzeit im südlichen Babylonien und im Golfgebiet*, Tübingen, 281-8.

Gatier, P.-L., Lombard, P. & al-Sindi, K. (2002), 'Greek inscriptions from Bahrain', *Arabian Archaeology and Epigraphy* 13: 223-33.

Grainger, J.D. (2002) *The Roman War of Antiochos the Great*, Leiden & Boston.

Hauser, R.S. (1999), 'Babylon in arsakidischer Zeit', in J. Renger (ed.), *Babylon: Focus mesopotamischer Geschichte, Wiege früher Gelehrsamkeit, Mythos in der Moderne*, Saarbrücken: 207-39.

Herling, A. & Salles, J.-F. (1993), 'Hellenistic cemeteries in Bahrain', in U. Finkbeiner (ed.), *Materialien zur Archäologie der Seleukiden- und Partherzeit im südlichen Babylonien und im Golfgebiet*, Tübingen: 161-82.

Herzfeld, E.E. (1934), *Archaeological History of Iran*, London.

Holt, F.L. (1993), *Alexander the Great and Bactria: The Formation of a Greek Frontier in Central Asia*, Leuven.

Hopkins, C. (1972), *Topography and Architecture of Seleucia on the Tigris*, Ann Arbor.

van Ingen, W. (1939), *Figurines from Seleucia on the Tigris*, Ann Arbor.

Invernizzi, A. (1993), 'Terracotta pinakes with erotic scenes from Seleucia on the Tigris', in A. Invernizzi & J.F. Salles (eds), *Arabia Antiqua: Hellenistic Centres around Arabia*, Rome: 155-65.

Invernizzi, A. (2004), *Seleucia al Tigri: le impronte di sigillo dagli archivi*, Alessandria.

Jeppesen, K. (1989), *Ikaros: The Hellenistic Settlement*, vol. 3: *The Sacred Enclosure in the Early Hellenistic Period*, Aarhus.

Kawami, T.S. (1987), *Monumental Art of the Parthian Period in Iran*, Acta Iranica 26, Leiden.

Keall, E.J. & Ciuk, K.E. (1991), 'Continuity of tradition in the pottery from Parthian Nippur', in K. Schippmann, A. Herling & J.-F. Salles (eds), *Golf-Archäologie: Mesopotamien, Iran, Kuwait, Bahrain, Vereinigte Arabische Emirate und Oman*, Buch am Erlbach: 57-70.

Koldewey, R. (1914), *The Excavations at Babylon*, London.

Kose, A. (1998), *Uruk, Architektur IV: von der Seleukiden- bis zur Sasanidenzeit*, Mainz am Rhein.

Kose, A. (2000): 'Das "Palais" auf Tell A von Girsu – Wohnstätte eines hellenistisch-parthischen Sammlers von Gudeastatuen', *Bagdhader Mitteilungen* 31: 377-426.

Kraeling, C.H. (1956), *The Excavations at Dura-Europos: conducted by Yale University and the French Academy of Inscriptions and Letters, Final report 8; Part 1, The Synagogue*, New Haven.

Kuhrt, A. & Sherwin-White, S. (1993), *From Samarkhand to Sardis: A New Approach to the Seleucid Empire*, London.

Lerner, J.D. (1999), *The Impact of Seleucid Decline on the Eastern Iranian Plateau*, Stuttgart.

Littleton, J. (1992), *Skeletons and Social Composition, Bahrain 300 BC-AD 250*, Oxford.

Loftus, W.K. (1857), *Travels and Researches in Chaldaea and Susiana*, London.

Bibliography

Lombard, P. & Salles, J.-F. (1984), *La nécropole de Janussan (Bahrain)*, Lyon.
McEwan, G.J.P. (1986), 'A Parthian campaign against Elymais in 77 BC', *Iran* 24: 91-4.
Martinez-Sève, L. (2002), *Les figurines de Suse*, Paris.
Martinez-Sève, L. (2002b), 'La ville de Suse à l'époque hellénistique', *Revue archéologique* 2002/1, no. 33: 31-53.
Mathiesen, H.E. (1982), *The Terracotta Figurines*, Copenhagen.
Mathiesen, H.E. (1992), *Sculpture in the Parthian Empire*, Aarhus.
Mittag, P.F. (2006), *Antiochus IV Epiphanes: Eine politische Biographie*, Berlin.
Negro Ponzi, M.M. (2005), 'Al-Ma'in: Problemi di Topografia', *Mesopotamia* XL: 145-69.
Neusner, J. (1969), *A History of the Jews in Babylonia I, The Parthian Period*, Brown Judaic Studies 62, Leiden.
Potts, D.T. (1990), *The Arabian Gulf in Antiquity*, vol. II: *From Alexander the Great to the Coming of Islam*, Oxford.
Potts, D.T. (1999), *The Archaeology of Elam*, Cambridge.
Price, M.J. (1991), *The Coinage in the Name of Alexander the Great and Philipp Arrhidaeus*, Zurich & London.
Rajak, T. (1988), 'The Parthians in Josephus', Josef Wiesehöfer (ed.), *Das Partherreich und seine Zeugnisse*, Stuttgart: 309-24.
Reuther, O. (1926), *Die Innenstadt von Babylon (Merkes)*, Dresden.
Rider, G. Le (1965), *Suse sous les Séleucides et les Parthes: les trouvailles monétaires et l'histoire de la ville*, Paris.
Roux, G. & Renger, J. (2005), *Irak in der Antike*, Mainz am Rhein.
Salles, J.-F. (1984), *Failaka, Fouilles Françaises 1983*, Lyon/Paris.
Schlumberger, D. (1969), *Der Hellenisierte Orient*, Baden-Baden.
Schmidt, J. (1978), 'Bemerkungen zum parthischen Haus in U XVIII, XXVIII', *Vorläufiger Bericht über die in dem Deutschen Archäologischen Institut aus den Mitteln der Deutschen Forschungsgemeinschaft unternommenen Ausgrabungen in Uruk-Warka 1970*, Berlin.
Schuol, M. (2000), *Die Charakene, Ein mesopotamisches Königreich in hellenistisch-parthischer Zeit*, Stuttgart.
Sellwood, D.G. (1980), *An Introduction to the Coinage of Parthia*, London.
van der Spek, R. (1998), 'Cuneiform documents of Parthian history', in Josef Wiesehöfer (ed.), *Das Partherreich und seine Zeugnisse*, Stuttgart: 205-58.
Ste. Croix, G.E.M. de (1981), *The Class Struggle in the Ancient Greek World*, London.
Strugnell, E. (2008), 'Thea Musa, Roman Queen of Parthia', *Iranica Antiqua* 43: 275-98.
Stucky, R. (ed.) (1977), *Trésors du musée de Bagdad*, Mainz am Rhein.
Vine, P. (ed.) (1993), *Bahrain National Museum*, London.
Wallenfels, R. (1994), *Hellenistic Seal Impressions*, Mainz am Rhein.
Wang Tao (2007), 'Parthia in China: a re-examination of the historical records', in V.S. Curtis & S. Stewart, *The Age of the Parthians: The Idea of Iran II*, London: 87-104.
Waterman, L. (1931a), *Preliminary Report upon the Excavations at Tel Umar, Iraq*, Ann Arbor.
Waterman, L. (1931b) *Second Preliminary Report upon the Excavations at Tel Umar, Iraq*, Ann Arbor.
Wetzel, F., Schmidt, E. & Mallwitz, A. (1957), *Das Babylon der Spätzeit*, Berlin.
Wiesehöfer, J. (1996), *Ancient Persia: from 550 BC to 650 AD*, London.

Bibliography

Wirth, F. (1934), *Römische Wandmalerei vom Untergang Pompejis bis ans Ende des dritten Jahrhunderts*, Berlin.

Wolski, J. (1988), 'Le titre de "roi des rois" dans l'idéologie monarchique des Arsacides', *Acta Antiqua Academiae Scientiarum Hungaricae*, fasc. 1-4: 159-66.

Wolski, J. (1993), *L'Empire des Arsacides*, Leuven.

Yonge, C.D. (1854), *The Deipnosophists, or, Banquet of the Learned of Athenaeus*, London.

Internet resources

http://www.parthia.com/Parthia.com (good website on the Parthians with long annotated list of literature)

John F. Hansman, 'Elymais', http://www.iranica.com/articles/elymais. Accessed 08/06/2010.

Index

Lightning Source UK Ltd.
Milton Keynes UK
UKHW021506070122
396779UK00005B/1087